The Future
of
Biological
Weapons

THE WASHINGTON PAPERS

... intended to meet the need for an authoritative, yet prompt, public appraisal of the major developments in world affairs.

President, CSIS: David M. Abshire

Series Editor: Walter Laqueur

Director of Publications: Nancy B. Eddy

Managing Editor: Donna R. Spitler

MANUSCRIPT SUBMISSION

The Washington Papers and Praeger Publishers welcome inquiries concerning manuscript submissions. Please include with your inquiry a curriculum vitae, synopsis, table of contents, and estimated manuscript length. Manuscript length must fall between 120 and 200 double-spaced typed pages. All submissions will be peer reviewed. Submissions to *The Washington Papers* should be sent to *The Washington Papers*; The Center for Strategic and International Studies; 1800 K Street NW; Suite 400; Washington, DC 20006. Book proposals should be sent to Praeger Publishers; One Madison Avenue; New York NY 10010.

The Future of Biological Weapons

Barend ter Haar

Foreword by Brad Roberts

Published with the Center for
Strategic and International Studies
Washington, D.C.

in Cooperation with the

Institute for the Study of Diplomacy
Georgetown University

PRAEGER

New York
Westport, Connecticut
London

Library of Congress Cataloging-in-Publication Data

Haar, Barend ter.
  The future of biological weapons / Barend ter Haar ; foreword by
Brad Roberts.
      p.   cm. — (The Washington papers, ISSN 0278-937X ; 151)
  "Published with the Center for Strategic and International
Studies, Washington, D.C., in cooperation with the Institute for the
Study of Diplomacy, Georgetown University."
  Includes bibliographical references and index.
  ISBN 0-275-94100-0 (HB). — ISBN 0-275-94101-9 (PB)
  1. Biological arms control—Verification.   2. Convention on the
Prohibition of the Development, Production, and Stockpiling of
Bacteriological (Biological) and Toxin Weapons and on Their
Destruction (1972)   I. CSIS.   II. Georgetown
University. Institute for the Study of Diplomacy.   III. Title.
IV. Series.
JX5133.C5H33   1991
341.7'35—dc20   91-12671

British Library Cataloging-in-Publication data is available.

Library of Congress Catalog Card Number: 91-12671
ISBN: 0-275-94100-0 (cloth)
        0-275-94101-9 (paper)

First published in 1991

Praeger Publishers, One Madison Avenue, New York, NY 10010
An imprint of Greenwood Publishing Group, Inc.

Printed in the United States of America

The paper used in this book complies with the Permanent
Paper Standard issued by the National Information Standards
Organization (Z39.48-1984).

10   9   8   7   6   5   4   3   2   1

Contents

Foreword

The Biological Weapons Convention (BWC) – officially the Convention on the Prohibition of the Development, Production, and Stockpiling of Bacteriological (Biological) and Toxin Weapons and on Their Destruction – was signed in Washington, London, and Moscow in April 1972 and entered into force three years later. It was the culmination of years of multilateral negotiations under the aegis of the United Nations, of initiatives by the Nixon Administration to renounce the use of biological agents of war and to disarm unilaterally in this area, and of the spirit of détente then flowering between East and West. Thus were biological agents – living organisms or infective materials derived from them that cause disease or death in humans, plants, or animals – banned from the arsenals of nations large and small. As of April 1991, 110 countries have become parties to the treaty.

The BWC, like the biological warfare issue itself, did not long remain at the center of public and international attention. A rapidly changing international environment and a dynamic, highly complex arms control and disarmament agenda shunted aside the issue. But the problem remains. In a series of periodic review conferences of states party to the BWC, concerns have emerged about the efficacy of the biological disarmament regime. These include the following:

First, the areas of science and technology covered by the BWC have undergone a virtual revolution since the treaty was written. Biotechnology has advanced in leaps and bounds since the negotiations of the 1960s and 1970s, with significant but little understood implications for biological warfare. Achievement of the biological disarmament regime was possible in part because of the extreme difficulty in using biological agents on the battlefield and the severe risks associated with their production, storage, and transfer even in times of peace. There is concern today that advances in the technologies related to these tasks may have diminished some of these perceived risks.

Second, the BWC lacks verification provisions. At the time, experts were skeptical about the feasibility of any measures to monitor compliance with treaty commitments, given the extensive scientific base and widespread civilian use of relevant technologies. There was also doubt about the necessity of verification provisions, given the perceptions of disutility and moral abhorrence attached to such weapons. Today, the debate about these issues has only sharpened.

Third, there is a highly politicized debate about the place of research oriented to defensive purposes. Many civilian advocates of disarmament are deeply skeptical of any research programs on biological agents and observe that the line between defensive and offensive purposes is quite fuzzy — essentially, a matter only of the quantities of agents in use in the laboratory. Yet others defend defensive research as an effective deterrent against cheating by a possible military opponent and as necessary in a regime lacking verification measures.

Fourth, the proliferation of offensive biological weapons programs is a growing concern. In the past couple of years, U.S. intelligence officials have reported the existence of such programs in at least 10 countries. The reported biological warfare capabilities of Iraq illustrate the problem. More countries may be seeking biological weapons either because of growing access to the technology, expertise, and material associated with their production or use or because of the limited but important military potential they represent.

Finally, there is the concern about actual treaty compliance. Soviet compliance is the sharpest but not the only concern. The U.S. intelligence community historically has been dissatisfied with the level of Soviet compliance, arguing that such events as the outbreak of anthrax at Sverdlovsk in 1979 and additional publicly unreportable evidence point to a sustained effort to circumvent treaty commitments. U.S. allegations of the use by Soviet and Soviet proxy forces of biological agents in Afghanistan and Southeast Asia in the 1970s and 1980s are the subject of continuing ferment – the so-called Yellow Rain debate – and although some alternative explanations have been offered, the issue has not yet closed. Soviet BWC compliance remains an issue despite the progress on other bilateral and multilateral arms control problems.

The cumulative effect of these concerns is reflected in waning confidence in the BWC as an effective instrument of international security. Some commentators decry it as the worst example of diplomatic naivete – as a foolish acquiescence to the sentimental disarmament mania of World War I vintage. Others see the issue as one of attempting to continue to work with and adapt the BWC to meet changing circumstances and new challenges. Sadly, some in the developing world consider the BWC irrelevant and perceive little stake in its effectiveness.

Efforts to bolster the BWC regime focus on the periodic review conferences (1980, 1986, 1991). The conference of 1986 emphasized doubts about treaty compliance and thus proposed a series of confidence-building measures. The 1991 conference, scheduled for September, is certain to highlight the modest success of these measures and begin a discussion of other measures to strengthen the regime.

This volume summarizes the issues confronting policymakers working to ensure that the BWC remains a bulwark against the proliferation and use of biological agents of warfare. Its author, Barend ter Haar, is one of the international diplomatic community's most respected experts on the control of biological weapons. His analysis provides the historical breadth and diplomatic depth necessary to an understanding of the current policy choices.

His proposals for modest reform of the existing biological disarmament regime, including some limited measures for verification beyond those implemented under the guise of confidence-building measures, will be central to the debate of the coming years about preserving effective control. The September 1991 review conference will debate the issues along some of the lines sketched here, but it will probably only make a tentative start at resolving the underlying problems.

It is reasonable to expect that effective biological disarmament – that is, a reversal of the trend toward proliferation and a resolution of problems of compliance – will be an ongoing challenge. The end of the winter 1991 war against Iraq brought worldwide relief that Iraqi chemical and biological weapons had not come into play. Yet the possibility alerted people to the risks associated with the proliferation of weapons of mass destruction and highlighted the international community's stake in effective biological disarmament. To a certain extent, the BWC's evolution is hostage to negotiations to achieve a parallel disarmament agreement in chemical agents; it is encouraging that negotiations for the Chemical Weapons Convention (CWC), under way since the conclusion of the BWC, may finally be reaching fruition. Given these factors, it is likely that the concerns relating to biological warfare and disarmament will increase, requiring international security experts to master a complex subject at the intersection of science, security, and diplomacy.

Brad Roberts
Director, Chemical Arms Control Project
Editor, *The Washington Quarterly*
The Center for Strategic and International Studies

About the Author

Barend ter Haar is a diplomat with the Netherlands Ministry of Foreign Affairs. He has been involved in efforts to strengthen the existing ban on biological weapons since 1982. In 1986 he participated in the Second Review Conference of the Biological Weapons Convention, and in 1987 he was head of the Netherlands delegation to the ad hoc meeting of experts to work out the confidence-building measures agreed at that review conference. As head of the nonnuclear arms control section of the Netherlands Ministry of Foreign Affairs, he participated in meetings on biological disarmament within the North Atlantic Treaty Organization (NATO) and in the framework of the European Political Cooperation. In 1989–1990 he spent a sabbatical at Georgetown University (Washington, D.C.) as an associate of the Institute for the Study of Diplomacy. Currently he is a member of the Netherlands delegation to NATO. He has published a number of articles on disarmament, mainly on chemical and biological weapons and on arms control agreements as prototypes for the enforcement of international environmental agreements.

Acknowledgments

I am grateful to the Institute for the Study of Diplomacy of Georgetown University, Washington, D.C., which gave me the opportunity to write this book during my sabbatical year there as a diplomatic research associate. I also thank Marie Chevrier, Jan Gerbrandy, Paul van den IJssel, Elisa Harris, Arend Meerburg, Matthew Meselson, Bob Mikulak, David Newsom, Graham Pearson, Julian Perry Robinson, and Brad Roberts for their helpful comments. The final responsibility is of course mine alone.

Summary

Today's worldwide spread of biotechnology allows the rapid production of large quantities of biological agents, thereby enabling most countries to produce biological warfare agents. Although the tactical utility of biological weapons remains questionable, some regimes seem interested in acquiring them to terrorize external and internal adversaries.

A policy of nonproliferation could slow this trend, but only temporarily, because the technology required for biological warfare agents is the same as needed for developing and producing medical and veterinary products. Only a comprehensive and worldwide ban can reverse the current trend toward biological warfare.

Countries concerned about the potential military implications of the developing life sciences negotiated the Geneva Protocol of 1925 to ban the use of bacteriological methods of warfare. The protocol did not, however, ban development and production of biological weapons. Several countries acquired a stockpile of these weapons, and Japan even used them.

The Biological Weapons Convention of 1972 was designed to correct these defects, but had its own shortcomings. It did not prohibit relevant activities categorically, because of their use for permitted purposes, and did not provide for measures to build confidence or to verify allegations.

In 1986 the Second Review Conference came as close to amending the convention as it possibly could by agreeing on a set of confidence-building measures (CBMs). This volume analyzes these first worldwide CBMs in some depth and recommends further measures to strengthen the convention, including

- initiatives to make the ban truly universal
- full implementation of CBMs
- regular meetings of parties to support such implementation
- extension of the scope of CBMs
- improvement of the processing of the exchanged data
- restrictions on the use of agents for protection (limitations on quantities, notification of open-air testing, et cetera)
- elaboration of a verification protocol that includes the opening for routine verification of all declared facilities and the acceptance of challenge inspections to occur anywhere, anytime.

Another recommendation extends the scope of the data exchange on laboratories to include all laboratories involved in protection against biological and toxin weapons and other laboratories and institutes of potential concern owing to the agents they handle (for example, agents that have been "weaponized" in the past) or the presence of relevant equipment (equipment, for example, for producing and conserving microorganisms, for harvesting, for long-term conservation of agents, or for high containment).

The Biological Weapons Convention is almost unverifiable in its present form; its scope depends on a party's intentions, and intentions are difficult to verify. Subjecting relevant items to obligatory declaration and quantitative limitations, however, could lay the foundation for an effective verification regime.

A verification regime can probably be modeled after the projected Chemical Weapons Convention. This volume discusses the principal concepts underlying the latter convention and suggests which lessons would apply to the Biological Weapons Convention. It should be remembered that biological agents differ fundamentally from chemical agents. Yet the feasibility and cost effectiveness of a verification regime can only be determined by developing such a regime and testing it in trial inspections.

Introduction

The main thesis of this volume is that the strength and credibility of the Biological Weapons Convention (BWC) can be significantly enhanced by adding a verification regime. The convention is almost unverifiable in its present form, but adding a few, relatively minor, obligations could make a verification regime possible.

To place the current predicament of the Biological Weapons Convention into perspective, this study begins with a short overview of its history. Next it analyzes in some detail the measures that have been agreed upon to strengthen the convention and the convention's current state. Finally the text discusses the lessons that can be drawn from the negotiations on a chemical weapons convention and the measures that could be taken to help the ban on biological weapons survive.

Biological agents of warfare were defined in a report of the secretary general of the United Nations as

> living organisms, whatever their nature, or infective material derived from them, which are intended to cause disease or death in man, animals or plants, and which depend for their effects on their ability to multiply in the person, animal or plant attacked.[1]

Chemical agents, in contrast, do not multiply but can be employed in warfare because of their direct toxic effects on man, animals, and plants. Toxins are a special category of chemical agents because they are produced by living organisms, although they do not reproduce themselves. They will be included in the scope of the Chemical Weapons Convention (CWC) being negotiated in Geneva, but because they are normally produced by biological organisms such as microbes, animals, and plants, and production therefore requires facilities that are very similar to facilities that produce biological agents, they were included in the scope of the Biological Weapons Convention. This study therefore deals with both biological agents and toxins.

The Future
of
Biological
Weapons

1

A Short History of Biological Arms Control

From the Geneva Protocol to the
Start of the Negotiations, 1925–1968

During many centuries more soldiers have been killed or disabled by disease than by the use of weapons. But if ever a war was won as a result of an epidemic, it was by accident rather than by design because the knowledge and technical power to manipulate disease for military purposes were virtually nonexistent. From time to time efforts were made to spread disease among adversaries by infecting water sources, for example, or by distributing infected goods, but biological warfare remained of marginal military interest. The destructive potential of biological weapons may be large, but the effects are very slow in comparison with both conventional weapons and other weapons of mass destruction. And above all, the effects are so difficult to predict that until well into this century very few military thinkers or practitioners seriously proposed developing biological weapons.

The development of the medical and biological sciences and the accompanying technologies helped bring many diseases under control, but it also opened the possibility of using these diseases for hostile purposes. As a result, international efforts got under way to ban the destructive use of this newly obtained knowledge and power. Thus began the interaction of the development of the life sciences, the application of these sciences to hostile purposes, and the efforts to ban such applications.

The first milestone in this interaction among life sciences, war, and politics was reached in 1925. In that year countries that were negotiating a protocol to reaffirm the prohibition of chemical weapons agreed on a Polish proposal to extend this prohibition "to the use of bacteriological methods of warfare."[1]

The Geneva Protocol is very important: It is the only international agreement that prohibits chemical warfare, and since its entry into force it has helped to limit the use of chemical weapons to relatively few cases. It probably also has helped prevent the use of biological weapons.

But the protocol has many limitations. They can be classified into three types:

Scope
• The protocol only prohibits the use in war. It could be argued that in other types of armed conflict, such as the fighting between pro- and anti-communist forces in Laos and Afghanistan, the protocol is not applicable.
• Some parties have reserved the right to use chemical and biological weapons against countries that are not party to the protocol.[2]
• Many parties have reserved the right to use chemical and biological weapons against parties whose armed forces or allies violate the protocol.[3]
• The protocol does not prohibit research, development, production, and stockpiling of these weapons and thus does not take away the threat of future use.
• It is not clear whether the protocol covers only lethal warfare agents or also covers nonlethal agents (such as tear gases).[4]
• It is not clear whether the protocol covers only the use of chemical and biological agents directly against hu-

mans or if it also covers hostile use of such agents against animals (for example, cattle) and plants.
   • The term "bacteriological" does not include all possible types of biological warfare agents. (In 1925 microorganisms such as viruses and rickettsias were not known. The scope of the protocol is nevertheless generally understood to encompass all types of microorganisms.)

Confidence building and verification
   • The protocol does not specify measures that would give parties confidence that other parties are honoring their obligations.
   • The protocol does not provide for ways to investigate doubts about compliance.[5]
   • The protocol does not have a mechanism to deal with violations.

Worldwide application
   • During the first decades of its existence, the protocol's effectiveness was limited because some major countries originally signed, but did not ratify, the protocol. Japan ratified in 1970 and the United States in 1975. And after the January 1989 Paris conference (where 14 countries declared their intent to become party to the protocol), its membership is virtually universal.

   Because of the limitations mentioned above, many countries, both parties and nonparties to the protocol, believed they should acquire a stockpile of chemical weapons to deter other countries from using them. The interest in biological weapons was much less, but for the same reasons that it was considered useful to add these weapons to the scope of the Geneva Protocol, several countries considered it wise to start research on them. Among those countries were both parties to the protocol such as the United Kingdom and nonparties such as Japan and the United States. The biological weapons programs of these countries are described here briefly to illustrate how real the prospect of biological weapons once was, not because these countries were the only ones interested. Other countries, such as France and very likely the Soviet Union, also developed a biological warfare capability or at least attempted it, as Germany did late in World War II.[6]

In February 1934 the United Kingdom decided to study the possibilities of biological warfare. Initially the program evolved slowly. In March 1937 a committee concluded that a large-scale attack with bacteria on Great Britain seemed unlikely but nevertheless urged the country to stockpile vaccines in preparation for a possible attack. The program was originally directed at defensive measures, but on January 2, 1942, the British government decided to acquire a capability to retaliate in kind against an attack with bacteria. For this purpose 5 million anthrax-filled cattle cakes were produced. The problems of delivering anthrax bombs were tested on Gruinard Island off the northwest coast of Scotland. As a result of these tests the island remained under control of the Ministry of Defence until it was effectively decontaminated in 1986 and 1987.[7] Similar tests were performed over Penclawdd Marsh in South Wales.[8]

Probably the most ambitious program to develop an offensive biological warfare capability was undertaken by Japan. In 1935 it started secretly researching biological weapons in Harbin in Manchuria.[9] Among the agents studied were anthrax, botulism, brucellosis, cholera, dysentery, plague, smallpox, and typhus. The agents were tested on prisoners. About 3,000 died during such experiments or, if they survived the tests, were killed afterward. Another unit was formed to study and produce animal and plant diseases.[10] This second unit was intended to have an annual production of 1,000 kilograms of anthrax (causing disease in both animals and man), 500 kilograms of glanders (causing disease in horses, communicable to man), and 100 kilograms of red rust (a plant disease), but these plans failed.[11]

The Japanese biological warfare program remained secret for a long time, and even now much is still unknown or uncertain. The record indicates that Japan used biological weapons several times.[12] One of the main problems of using biological warfare agents proved to be bringing a sufficient amount of infectious material to the victims. Conventional bombing techniques did not work, because the heat and the pressure of the explosion killed the microbes before they could do any harm. Many unconventional techniques were tried. Porcelain bombs were developed, for example, that could contain about 30,000 infected fleas.[13] In this manner, plague, tetanus, and anthrax could be dispersed at the front. Bombs with typhoid and dysentery were considered for attacks in the rear. Anthrax-infected chocolates also were made.[14] The most effective method for dispersal was by personnel on the ground. During operations that probably took place in the second half of 1942, cholera, dysentery, typhoid, plague, anthrax, and paratyphoid were spread by special troops who were left behind when Japanese forces retreated. The Chinese losses were described as "inestimable."[15] The casualties among Japanese troops, however, also were very heavy. More than 10,000 Japanese soldiers fell ill when they overran a contaminated area, probably because the regular Japanese soldiers were not told about the use of biological warfare agents.

The United States received its first indications of the Japanese interest in biological warfare in 1939, when Japan tried to acquire a strain of yellow fever virus in the United States.[16] The United States started biological warfare research in 1941 within its Chemical Warfare Service.[17] In February 1942 a committee appointed by the National Academy of Sciences recommended the following:

> The value of biological warfare will be a debatable question until it has been clearly proven or disproven by experience. Such experience may be forthcoming. The wise assumption is that any method which appears to offer advantages to a nation at war will be vigorously employed by that nation. There is but one logical course to pursue, namely to study the possibilities of such warfare from every angle, make every preparation for reducing its effectiveness and thereby reduce the

likelihood of its use. In order to plan such preparation,
it is advantageous to take the point of view of the ag-
gressor and to give careful attention to the characteristics which a biologic offensive might have.[18]

During 1942 and 1943 the biological warfare program
expanded. During World War II about 4,000 people were
involved in the program.[19] At the end of 1943, work started
on 500-pound anthrax bombs and on botulinum toxin
bombs. Other agents under consideration were probably
brucellosis, psittacosis, tularemia, and glanders.[20] A major
reason for this development was the fear that Germany
might start using these weapons. After World War II the
United States obtained a large amount of information
about the Japanese program and continued its own program. Apart from Fort Detrick, the center for biological
weapons research, about 300 universities, research institutes, and corporations were involved.[21] When in 1969 President Richard M. Nixon decided to destroy all U.S. biological
weapons, at least 10 different biological and toxin warfare
agents were available.[22]

During World War II, the allied powers had agreed that
Korea, which had been ruled by Japan since 1910, would
again be independent. The temporary occupation of the
northern half of the country by the Soviet Union and of the
southern half by the United States, however, resulted in a
Communist northern part and a Western-oriented southern
part. In 1949 the occupation troops were withdrawn, and in
June 1950 the North attacked the South. The Chinese seat
in the United Nations (UN) was still taken by the Taiwan
Republic of China, and the Soviet Union was boycotting the
Security Council at that time. The United States was therefore able to get the support of the Security Council for
military measures against the aggressors.[23] An army was
sent to Korea consisting of forces from 16 nations. The
contribution of the United States was, however, predomi-
nant. After years of heavy fighting, a truce was signed in

1953 that left the situation largely as it was before the war started.

In May 1951 the North Korean government accused U.S. forces of using bacteriological weapons. Similar accusations were made during 1952. The U.S. Army was said to have distributed large amounts of infected insects in the rear of the North Korean and Chinese forces to spread plague, cholera, typhus, and other contagious diseases.[24] The allegations were supported by reports of investigations conducted by committees the Communist governments had appointed unilaterally. These same governments also gave much publicity to what they claimed to be confessions of prisoners of war. The United States denied the accusations and proposed that the International Committee of the Red Cross investigate the facts on the spot. But a draft resolution of the Security Council to this effect was vetoed by the Soviet Union on the grounds that the Security Council was not willing to allow representatives of the People's Republic of China and North Korea to take part in the deliberations and that the International Red Cross Committee was not impartial. Neither the Soviet Union nor North Korea nor the Chinese People's Republic suggested an alternative manner to investigate the facts. They also refused an offer of the World Health Organization (WHO) to help control the reported epidemics.[25]

Because the Security Council could not act on this issue,[26] the General Assembly (where the Soviet Union did not have veto power) decided on April 23, 1953, to set up a commission composed of Brazil, Egypt, Pakistan, Sweden, and Uruguay to investigate the charges.[27] The commission should be enabled to travel freely throughout North and South Korea, China, and Japan and should be allowed to examine all prisoners of war who were alleged to have made confessions about bacteriological warfare. Such examination should take place in a neutral area, and the examined prisoners should remain under the custody of the commission until the end of the war. But the whole exercise depended on the acceptance of all concerned governments;

because the Communist governments did not accept the investigation, it was never conducted.

There is little reason to believe that the allegations against the U.S. armed forces were based on trustworthy evidence, and the whole affair might not have been worth mentioning if it were not such a good example of the fundamental need for openness, both to refute and to substantiate accusations.

Technological and scientific developments during the nineteenth and the beginning of the twentieth century made biological warfare a distinct possibility. The Geneva Protocol of 1925 was an important milestone in the effort to make sure this knowledge was applied only to peaceful purposes. Even so, the Geneva Protocol had many shortcomings. As science and technology developed after 1925, these shortcomings became more apparent. Biological weapons were developed, produced, and even used. Although the military utility of these weapons remained questionable, the danger grew that the restraints on use would erode.

Negotiations on the Convention, 1968–1972

After World War II ended, great expectations existed about the prospects of disarmament. During the 1950s and early 1960s negotiations were directed at general and complete disarmament. Special attention was given to the elimination of weapons of mass destruction, which were defined to include nuclear weapons as well as chemical and biological weapons, but no detailed discussion took place on the elimination of biological and chemical weapons.[28] The negotiations on a comprehensive approach to disarmament including the elimination of all weapons of mass destruction eventually foundered.

Gradually it became clear that negotiations on comprehensive disarmament had little chance of success and that, if concrete results were required, the disarmament negotiations should strive for more limited objectives. This resulted in 1963 in the Partial Test Ban Treaty and in 1968 in the nuclear Non-Proliferation Treaty. At the same time the interest in the problem of chemical and biological weapons grew, because the United States used chemical agents in Vietnam. According to the United States, the agents used (tear gases and herbicides) did not fall within the definition of chemical weapons, and their use therefore did not violate the probition on the use of chemical weapons.[29] As a result of this debate, renewed attention was drawn to the limitations of the Geneva Protocol. Initially proposals to amend the protocol, such as the draft resolution proposed by Malta and the Netherlands in the Twenty-second Session of the UN General Assembly in 1967, were rejected by the socialist countries.[30] They claimed that the protocol was sufficiently clear and that discussions about amendments would undermine the protocol and legitimize the methods of warfare used by the United States in Vietnam.[31]

The UK Proposal

In August 1968 the United Kingdom delegation introduced a working document in the Eighteen-Nation Disarmament Committee (ENDC).[32] It proposed a new convention for the prohibition of microbiological methods of warfare that would supplement, but not supersede, the Geneva Protocol. It suggested that the questions of biological and chemical methods of warfare be separated. Biological weapons were considered to be of far less military relevance than chemical weapons but were viewed with even more abhorrence. A comprehensive ban of biological weapons was within reach because a verification regime was not a sine qua non. But a complete ban on chemical weapons would be much more difficult to agree upon because chemical weapons had been used and stockpiled, and many states would therefore not be willing to ban these weapons unless a verification regime assured them that other parties would comply. The new convention would proscribe hostile use of microbiological agents against "man, other animals, or crops" and would also ban research aimed at the production of such micro-biological warfare agents.[33] All research work that might be suspected of violating the convention should "be open to international investigation if so required."[34] "In the knowledge that strict processes of verification are not possible," it was suggested that a body of experts, established under the auspices of the United Nations, might investigate allegations about noncompliance.[35] Parties would undertake to cooperate fully in any investigation.

In reaction to the British proposal, Sweden suggested the concept of "verification by challenge." Sweden had proposed this concept two years earlier in a statement on "verification by consent" concerning an agreement to verify a ban on underground nuclear testing.[36] The idea was that if doubts arose about compliance, the suspected party would like to dispel such doubts by extending an invitation to visit the site in question. If the suspected party would not take the initiative for such an "inspection by invitation," the party with strong doubts about compliance should have an opportunity to challenge the other party to issue such an invitation.[37] This concept later played an important role in the negotiations on a chemical weapons ban.

At the end of its 1968 session, the ENDC decided to put the questions of bacteriological and chemical warfare formally on its agenda. The ENDC also recommended that the secretary general of the United Nations appoint a group of experts to study the effects of the use of these weapons.[38] In his annual report for 1967–1968, the secretary general welcomed this recommendation but suggested the scope of the study be widened to "the dangers of chemical and biological weapons."[39] The Geneva Protocol spoke about "bacteriological" methods of warfare, because other types of microbiological organisms, such as viruses, were not yet known. Because nobody disputed that the protocol was also meant to cover other biological organisms than bacteria, the secretary general considered it wise to use the broader term "biological." The socialist countries, however, did not want to deviate from the terminology of the Geneva Protocol. The resolution of the General Assembly that endorsed the recommendations of both the ENDC and the secretary general avoided the problem.[40]

The group of experts submitted a unanimous report to the secretary general.[41] For the subject of the study (next to chemical weapons), the somewhat clumsy compromise wording "bacteriological (biological) weapons" was found. This was in keeping with the wordings of the Geneva Protocol but indicated that "bacteriological" should be interpreted broadly. The report concluded that the effect of large-scale use of certain chemical and biological agents is unpredictable and could have irreversible effects.[42] The group also pointed out that "any country could develop or acquire, in one way or another, a capability in this type of warfare, despite the fact that this could prove costly."[43] The report was generally acclaimed and proved to be an important foundation for the negotiations on banning biological and chemical weapons.

On July 10, 1969, the United Kingdom introduced a draft convention for the prohibition of biological methods of warfare in the ENDC, in combination with a draft Security Council resolution.[44] The draft convention was largely along the lines of the working document the United Kingdom submitted the year before, but the proposed verification measures were different. The idea of opening research for international investigation had been dropped. And instead of establishing a body of experts to investigate allegations about noncompliance, a distinction was now made between allegations of use of biological weapons and other allegations. If a party believed that biological weapons had been used against it, it could request the secretary general to investigate its complaint;[45] in all other cases (for example, if it were threatened with biological weapons or suspected the production of biological weapons) the party would have to ask the Security Council to consider its complaint.[46] In the accompanying Security Council resolution, the Security Council would request the secretary general to take measures that would enable him to investigate complaints about use lodged with him directly and other complaints about noncompliance if so requested by the Security Council.

On September 19, 1969, the Soviet Union, together with some of its allies, submitted to the General Assembly a draft convention that differed from the British draft in several aspects.[47] It covered both biological and chemical weapons but did not prohibit research or use. Neither did it provide for international verification nor for a mechanism to deal with complaints about compliance.[48]

The socialist countries claimed that the fact that chemical weapons had been used and were stockpiled did not require a separate ban on biological weapons but, on the contrary, increased the urgency of dealing with chemical weapons. Agreement on international verification would be impracticable anyway, so that was not a good reason to postpone a ban on chemical weapons. The nonaligned countries in the Conference of the Committee on Disarmament (CCD) also maintained that biological and chemical weapons should be treated together.[49] But both Sweden and Morocco suggested that a ban on chemical weapons might require a separate verification regime.

Meanwhile in the United States, a policy review brought important changes in the U.S. position and even measures of unilateral disarmament. On November 25, 1969, President Nixon announced that he would submit the Geneva Protocol to the Senate for ratification and that the United States would unilaterally renounce biological warfare.[50] Research would be limited to defensive measures, such as immunization, and existing stocks of biological warfare agents would be destroyed.

On February 14, 1970, the United States extended its renunciation of biological weapons to toxins. Although toxins are chemical substances, they are usually produced by living organisms. A production plant of toxin warfare agents would therefore be very similar to a plant of biological warfare agents. To prevent any doubts about compliance, the United States therefore proposed that toxins be brought under the scope of a biological weapons convention.[51] In anticipation of such an agreement, the United States unilaterally renounced the use of toxins as a method of warfare and declared that it would destroy all stocks except for quantities needed for defensive research, such as methods to improve immunization.

In 1970 both the United Kingdom and the socialist countries introduced revised versions of their draft conventions. In the revised draft the United Kingdom introduced, toxins were brought within the scope of the convention.[52] The most important addition in the new Soviet draft was a provision that would allow parties to lodge complaints about compliance with the Security Council.[53] Parties would undertake "to co-operate" in investigations "which the Security Council may undertake." This came closer to the British draft. But whereas according to the Soviet draft the Security Council would undertake investigations, the United Kingdom proposed that "the Secretary-General and his authorized representatives" carry out inspections. In the latter case, the permanent members of the Security Council would miss the opportunity to interfere with an inspection.

The CCD spent much time in 1970 on the question of verifying a ban on biological and chemical weapons. Among the concepts discussed were reporting of data to an international agency and verification by challenge.[54] Most of the attention was directed at verifying a ban on chemical weapons; little thought was given to the possibility of verifying a ban on biological weapons. In a working document on verification of a ban of chemical and biological weapons, Canada stated that only a verification by complaint procedure seemed feasible.[55] It would be futile to devise other verification mechanisms. The most logical solution would be that governments would accept "the risks inherent in verification through a complaint procedure for biological warfare."[56]

Remaining Differences

In 1971 the Soviet Union agreed to deal separately with biological and toxin weapons.[57] Disagreement remained, however, on including a prohibition against use. The United Kingdom pressed for inclusion because of the many short-comings of the Geneva Protocol. The socialist countries maintained that including a prohibition on use would un-dermine the Geneva Protocol and that such a prohibition would be less relevant anyway because use would be impos-sible if all existing stocks had been destroyed and produc-tion of new stocks were prohibited. The Western countries ultimately acquiesced to noninclusion, provided that the text of the convention make clear its purpose of excluding any possibility of use.

Another difference of opinion concerned the Security Council's role in case of complaints.[58] Finally agreement was reached on the wording that the Security Council may "initiate" an investigation.[59] This gave the Soviet Union the power to veto the initiation of an investigation but opened the possibility that a body other than the Security Council would be charged with the actual conduct of an investigation.

On August 5, 1971, the socialist countries and the United States introduced separate but identical draft con-ventions in the CCD.[60] During the following two months, the CCD considered many amendments. On September 28, 12 Western and socialist countries jointly submitted a re-vised draft convention.[61] To make clear that no exceptions or reservations on the ban would be allowed, the basic com-mitment in Article 1 was extended with the words "never in any circumstances." Also in Article 1 the phrase "whatever their origin or method of production" was added to "toxins" to clarify that all toxins would fall within the scope of the ban, even when they were produced by chemical synthesis. Article 5 was enlarged with a provision that consultation and cooperation also may be undertaken through international procedures within the framework of the United Nations.

The CCD submitted this revised draft without further changes to the UN General Assembly, and the Convention on the Prohibition of the Development, Production, and Stockpiling of Bacteriological (Biological) and Toxin Weapons and on Their Destruction was opened for signature on April 10, 1972. Interestingly, around that time the foundation was laid for modern biotechnology by the discovery of recombinant DNA techniques. It would take several years, however, for a discussion to get under way on the implications of these techniques for biological warfare.

Assessing the BWC

The Biological Weapons Convention (BWC) made up for many of the shortcomings of the Geneva Protocol, as far as biological and toxin agents are concerned.[62] Although the convention did not explicitly prohibit the use of these agents, the obligation in Article 1 "never in any circumstances to develop, produce, stockpile or otherwise acquire or retain" such agents "of types and in quantities that have no justification for prophylactic, protective or other peaceful purposes" left no doubt that their use would never be permitted. The wording of Article 1 made clear that the prohibition is not limited to war or to conflicts between parties but is valid "in any circumstances," leaving no room for reservations. Even if a party were attacked with biological weapons, that party would not be allowed to retaliate in kind. Under such exceptional circumstances, however, a party would have the right to withdraw from the convention after giving all others parties and the Security Council notice of such withdrawal three months in advance.[63]

Another weakness of the protocol was the use of the word "bacteriological," which implies that microorganisms like viruses and rickettsias were not covered. The convention prevented such misunderstanding by using the words "bacteriological (biological) weapons" in the title and preamble and the phrase "microbial or other biological agents" in Article 1.

In comparison with the 1925 protocol, the provision in Article 6 that parties might lodge a complaint with the Security Council, and that the Security Council might initiate an investigation, could be considered a step in the right direction, but it has become clear since that these procedures have not prevented or solved doubts about compliance.

Like the limitations of the Geneva Protocol, the weaknesses of the convention fall into three categories (discussed in later chapters):

Scope
  • The convention does not prohibit research on biological weapons and allows development, production, and stockpiling in quantities justified for "protective or other peaceful purposes" without setting a clear and objective limit on such quantities.
  • The convention does not explicitly cover biological and toxin agents directed against animals and plants.

Confidence building and verification
  • Routine measures to give confidence in compliance are missing.
  • Doubts about compliance cannot effectively be investigated.
  • The convention cannot deal with violations.

Worldwide application
  • Several relevant countries did not become party.[64]

A comparison of this list with the list of limitations of the Geneva Protocol illustrates the accomplishments of the Biological Weapons Convention. But the remaining weaknesses are very serious.

In 1972 the military relevance of biological weapons was still considered to be so small that most countries could agree on a comprehensive ban on biological weapons that included several important flaws. The main problems were the lack of measures to provide confidence in compliance, the absence of an effective verification regime in case of doubts about compliance, and the fact that not all relevant countries became party. It is interesting to note that several of the concepts dropped during the negotiations – such as openness of research to allow investigation and verification of allegations regarding production and stockpiling of biological weapons – are now being considered again to strengthen the convention.

Entry into Force and the First Review Conference, 1972–1980

The Biological Weapons Convention entered into force on March 26, 1975. A few weeks earlier, on March 4, the U.S. delegation to the CCD had declared that its biological and toxin weapons had been destroyed and the production installations had been converted to peaceful purposes.[65] The representatives of the United Kingdom and the Soviet Union declared that their countries did not possess biological weapons.[66] The period between the signing of the convention and the First Review Conference was not marked by any major controversy, but concerns were expressed that the development of genetic engineering techniques might lead to new biological warfare agents. The number of parties steadily grew, but China and France remained unwilling to become party to the convention. Neither country had been involved in the negotiations of the convention, and France was very critical about the absence of verification procedures.[67]

Scientific and Technological Developments

The First Review Conference was held in Geneva from March 3 to 21, 1980.[68] Experts of the three depositary powers (United Kingdom, the United States, and the Soviet

Union) had prepared a report for the conference on new scientific and technological developments.[69] The report discussed developments such as recombinant DNA techniques but concluded that it was unlikely that agents produced by genetic manipulation would have advantages over known natural agents "sufficient to provide compelling new motives for illegal production or military use in the foreseeable future." Nevertheless, developments in genetic engineering "should be followed closely and periodically re-evaluated." The report also noted that the eradication of such infectious diseases as smallpox could result in widespread vulnerability to the use of such agents in warfare. It concluded in a reassuring tone:

> The language of the Convention fully covers all agents which could result from application of recombinant DNA techniques or of any of the other new developments discussed in this paper. . . . From a scientific and technological standpoint, the developments discussed in this paper, which are directed to peaceful purposes, do not appear to alter substantially capabilities or incentives for the development or production of biological or toxin weapons.

The conclusion that the convention covers all possible new agents was not disputed and was adopted in the final declaration of the conference.[70] But not everybody was convinced that nobody would ever be interested in using biological weapons. The Netherlands observer-delegation, for example, on March 13 pointed out the possibility that new diseases could be used against island populations.

Proposals for Amendment

Sweden, backed by many nonaligned states, expressed concern about the effectiveness of the convention's complaints procedure and proposed the establishment of a permanent consultative committee consisting of representatives of parties.[71] This consultative committee would arrange fact-find-ings, including on-site visits. Only when such procedures had been exhausted should a party lodge a complaint with the Security Council.

Sweden also proposed an amendment that would make a request to the Security Council to initiate an investigation considered a procedural matter. This status would deprive the Security Council's permanent members of the option to use their veto power.

Agreed-upon Interpretations

The socialist countries strongly opposed the proposals for amendment. They stipulated that it would be ill-advised to amend a treaty that was operating well. Most Western countries believed that the procedures in Articles 5 and 6 for consultation and complaints should be strengthened. But they doubted that amendment would help because several parties would not accept the amendments, thereby creating two categories of parties. This situation would weaken rather than strengthen the convention. Another reason to be very reluctant about amendments was the precedent this would set for the Non-Proliferation Treaty.

The United Kingdom therefore suggested that instead of amending the convention, the review conference would in its final declaration build upon Article 5 by interpreting the phrase "through appropriate international procedures within the framework of the United Nations" as implying the automatic establishment of a consultative committee of experts. Eventually it was agreed to incorporate a sentence in the final declaration that the procedures of Article 5 "include, *inter alia*, the right of any State Party subsequently to request that a consultative meeting open to all States Parties be convened at expert level."[72]

Exchange of Information

The conference also made a beginning in inviting parties to take confidence-building measures. Article 2 of the final declaration, which was adopted by consensus as part of the final document of the conference, states that parties should make voluntary declarations that they never have possessed agents and equipment for biological warfare or that, having possessed them, the parties have destroyed them or diverted them to peaceful purposes. On the suggestion of the United Kingdom, parties were invited to make available to the United Nations Center for Disarmament the texts of national legislation or regulatory measures that they have introduced to implement the convention (Art. 4). Several parties, such as Belgium, Canada, Finland, and the United States, supported the British proposal,[73] but according to the United Nations Department for Disarmament Affairs, by the spring of 1990 only four parties had implemented this provision.[74]

The Convention Threatened, 1980–1986

Sverdlovsk

When analyzing the photographs made by a reconnaissance satellite of a military complex at the southern edge of Sverdlovsk (1,350 kilometers east of Moscow), U.S. experts noted such unusual characteristics as pens for animals, cooling systems, and an air-conditioning system (very unusual for a military establishment in that part of the world). The security of the complex was very heavy. The U.S. experts thought it could be a biological weapons plant.

On April 2, 1979, Sverdlovsk was hit by an anthrax epidemic. Reports on the disaster started to appear in the West only much later. In January 1980 *Possev*, a periodical of Soviet emigrants, contained an article in which the anthrax epidemic was attributed to an explosion. According to the article, the first victims had been brought to the hospital on April 4, 1979, with temperatures of 42 degrees centigrade and had died within three hours after hospitalization. As many as 1,000 people were reported to have died. On March 18, 1980 (just a few days before the First

Review Conference ended and only one day after it had bilaterally asked the Soviet Union for an explanation), the U.S. Department of State confirmed reports that Sverdlovsk might have been struck by a deadly biological agent. Might anthrax have been present in quantities inconsistent with the Biological Weapons Convention? In other words, was the epidemic the result of an accident at a biological weapons plant?

On March 21, 1980, after the final document of the First Review Conference had been adopted, the representative of the United States declared that his country had started consultations with the Soviet Union regarding this incident. The delegation of the Soviet Union, in a somewhat nettled manner, pointed out that an anthrax epidemic had occurred in Sverdlovsk because of the consumption of infected meat purchased on the black market.

Anthrax is indeed endemic in the Sverdlovsk region, but according to the United States, the victims' symptoms did not point to common intestinal anthrax but to inhalation anthrax, which corresponds with the theory of an accident at a biological weapons plant. But the conclusion about the type of anthrax could not be substantiated by the available evidence or by the available knowledge about different forms.[75] A doctor who headed the intensive therapy department of a hospital in Sverdlovsk at the time of the epidemic recalled that most of the patients were men around 40 years old and concluded that it was the doing of genetic engineering that created a highly effective bacteria that hit only residents of a certain age capable of carrying weapons.[76] A different explanation of the peculiar composition of the victims is that the infected meat was bought and eaten by those who could afford to buy meat on the black market: male workers. Although the evidence was insufficient to prove that the epidemic resulted from an accident at a military biological weapons research center, the secretiveness of the Soviet Union did little to allay such suspicions.

At the Second Review Conference the USSR was some-

what more forthcoming on the subject. Soviet delegate pro-
fessor Nikolai Antonov gave a detailed description of the
anthrax outbreak but was still unable to remove all doubts.
Efforts to answer all remaining questions have continued.
In April 1988, for example, Soviet experts visited the United States and gave additional information about the outbreak.[77] But so far no consensus has been reached about
what happened in 1979. Thanks to the exchange of information on biological weapons laboratories, it is now clear that
the suspected facility was indeed a military biological weapons research center. The institute was engaged in research
and development and production of vaccines to protect
troops and civilians against a number of dangerous infec-
tions.[78] This work was said to have been stopped in 1986
and never resumed. Anthrax was probably stockpiled at the
institute, but as long as the quantities could be justified for
research and the production of vaccines, this supply would
have been in accordance with the convention. The critical
question remains what the facility is doing now.

Yellow Rain

In 1975, after the fall of Saigon, the neutral government of
Laos was succeeded by a Communist government backed
by Vietnamese forces. In 1978 Vietnam invaded Cambodia
and installed a pro-Vietnamese regime. A year later the
Soviet Union invaded Afghanistan. The fighting in these
three countries continued. In Laos the central government
and Vietnamese forces tried to subdue mountain tribes
such as the Hmong in northern Laos. In Cambodia the war
continued between the Vietnamese army and the Khmer
Rouge, and in Afghanistan Soviet forces fought against the
Mujaheddin-e-Khalq, a loose coalition of tribes and group-
ings that opposed central Communist government.

   At the end of the 1970s, stories started to turn up
about the use of chemical weapons in Laos and Cambodia.
From 1981 onward the stories concentrated on toxin weap-

ons.[79] The details of the stories usually differed widely. It was alleged that all possible types of dispersal were used, ranging from shell fire to spraying by different types of aircraft. The color of the agent also differed: white, black, blue, gray, green, red, silver, but most often yellow.[80] Most of the stories originated with the Hmong, a mountain tribe in northern Laos that dubbed the mysterious agent "yellow rain." Around 1980, comparable stories popped up about Soviet troops using chemical weapons in Afghanistan.[81] Because the Soviet Union was directly or indirectly involved in all three countries, suspicions grew that it was behind the use of these weapons. Such use was not a direct violation of the Geneva Protocol, because at that time Afghanistan, Cambodia, Laos, and Vietnam were not party to the protocol, but it would have certainly been a violation of a generally recognized rule of customary international law that prohibits the first use of chemical weapons in any conflict.[82] And if, as was suspected, the Soviet Union was assisting Vietnam in using toxin weapons, this would have been a violation of Article 3 of the Biological Weapons Convention, in which parties undertake not to help any state acquire biological or toxin weapons. The use of toxin weapons by Soviet armed forces in Afghanistan clearly would have violated Article 1, which prohibits possession of biological weapons.

All the mentioned states denied the accusations and vehemently opposed a UN General Assembly resolution in which the secretary general was requested to carry out an investigation. The resolution was nevertheless adopted.[83] Although its mandate was extended in 1981 by a year, the group of experts appointed by the secretary general did not reach clear conclusions.[84] This was mainly because the group could not travel to the territories where the attacks allegedly had occurred. The governments of Afghanistan and Laos would not admit the group into their territory, and the authorities of "Democratic Kampuchea" could not guarantee the security of the experts in Cambodia.[85] The experts therefore had to base their conclusions mainly on circumstantial evidence provided by refugees in Thailand, among others. In its final report, published on December 1, 1982, the group concluded that although "it could not state that these allegations had been proven, nevertheless it could not disregard the circumstantial evidence suggestive of the possible use of some sort of toxic chemical substance in some instances."[86]

Disputed Evidence

On September 13, 1981, Secretary of State Alexander Haig declared that the United States had evidence that toxin weapons had been used in Afghanistan, Laos, and Cambodia. These allegations were later bolstered by a number of reports.[87] Samples of so-called yellow rain were reported to contain trichothecene mycotoxins, a toxin generated by a mold that occurs in the Soviet Union but was not known to occur in Southeast Asia. But many experts considered the evidence submitted by the United States inconclusive. The United States was never able to provide proof that was both completely reliable and convincing. Conspicuously missing was any trace of the equipment that would have been used to deliver the agents.

The circumstantial evidence seemed nevertheless strong. How could all the strange facts be explained unless indeed something strange had happened? But one by one credible alternative explanations of all the facts were suggested. The toxins on which the allegations concentrated, for example, turned out to occur naturally in Southeastern Asia, so even their presence in samples (which was questioned) did not irrefutably prove that toxin weapons had been used. The fact that most stories about yellow rain originate with the Hmong could possibly be explained: stories about yellow rain, as a kind of evil power, seem to form part of the culture of the Hmong.[88] The actual occurrence of something like yellow rain could very well be explained as the result of a whole colony of bees getting rid of the pollen they consumed.[89] Furthermore, the manner in which interviews with the supposed victims had been conducted proved to be contestable.[90]

Procedures for Investigation
of Alleged Use

As a result of the yellow rain controversy in 1982, a number of Western and nonaligned countries proposed that the UN General Assembly request the secretary general to devise procedures for effectively investigating reports concerning violations of the prohibition on using chemical and biological weapons. The draft resolution also asked the secretary general to investigate any such reports that might be brought to his attention by any member state and to compile lists of qualified experts and laboratories that might assist in carrying out such investigations. The socialist countries opposed the proposal because in their view it was up to the parties, not to the General Assembly, to supplement the protocol. The resolution was nevertheless adopted.[91] The preparation for future investigations proved useful even before the report was finished, when, in the beginning of 1984, the secretary general sent the first group of experts to investigate reports on the use of chemical weapons in the war between Iraq and Iran.[92]

In 1987 the General Assembly adopted a resolution that in substance was almost identical to the above-mentioned resolution of 1982.[93] But in contrast to 1982, this time the resolution was adopted by consensus. Twenty-six countries replied to the resolution and informed the secretary general of available experts and laboratories.[94] The report of the group of experts established in pursuance of the resolution was submitted to the General Assembly on October 4, 1989.[95] Adoption of these resolutions, especially the latter's adoption because it was by consensus, accomplished what the United Kingdom and other Western countries had vainly aspired toward during the negotiations on the convention – namely, the right of the secretary general to initiate investigations of alleged use of chemical and biological weapons.

Lessons for the Convention

The main conclusion most parties drew from the controversy around Sverdlovsk and yellow rain was that the procedures for consultation, cooperation, and investigations were clearly insufficient. In the autumn of 1982 Sweden and a number of other nonaligned and neutral countries therefore introduced a draft resolution in the UN General Assembly recommending that the parties to the convention hold "a special conference as soon as possible to establish a flexible, objective and non-discriminatory procedure to deal with issues concerning compliance. . . . "Again the socialist countries were opposed. They stated that this proposal was another attempt to undermine existing agreements. The Soviet Union added that no reason existed to question the effectiveness of the consultation mechanism provided in the convention. Only India, however, joined the socialist bloc in voting against the resolution.[96]

After the adoption of the resolution, Sweden asked the three depositaries of the convention to convene such a special conference as soon as possible.[97] The Soviet Union remained opposed but left open the possibility that proposals for amending the convention would be discussed at the next review conference. The First Review Conference had decided that the next such conference would be held "not earlier than 1985 and, in any case, not later than 1990."[98] Sweden therefore proposed to convene the Second Review Conference as soon as possible.[99] Subsequently Norway proposed to convene the review conference in 1986.[100] A majority of the parties supported this proposal.[101]

The anthrax epidemic in Sverdlovsk and the allegations about yellow rain might seem pure anecdotes illustrating the atmosphere of mistrust between the United States and the Soviet Union, but they were much more than that. Confidence in the convention was undermined, and especially in the United States, the question was raised as to whether the convention served any useful purpose or only provided a false sense of security. What would be the convention's future if confidence in compliance could not be restored? At least parties became convinced of the necessity of greater openness—not only in cases of such allegations but as a matter of routine—about relevant research centers, such as the laboratory in Sverdlovsk, and about unusual outbreaks of diseases, such as the anthrax epidemic.

The Second Review Conference, 1986

The Second Review Conference, which was held in Geneva September 8–26, 1986, promised to be eventful, because the United States could be expected to repeat its accusations that the Soviet Union had violated the convention by its biological weapon activities in Sverdlovsk, by using toxin weapons in Afghanistan, and by assisting Vietnam to use these weapons in Southeast Asia.[102] Very few countries were able or willing to support these accusations, but most were now convinced that the procedures for consultation and verification of the convention were not sufficient. If doubts about compliance were allowed to remain, they would eventually undermine the convention. The procedures for consultation and verification should therefore be strengthened.

The United States reacted differently. It considered the unwillingness of the socialist bloc to disprove the evidence that pointed toward violations and the U.S. difficulty in convincing other governments its accusations were well founded as proof that the convention was basically flawed and in fact beyond repair—flawed because of the lack of verification procedures and beyond repair because effective verification would be impossible. The United States thought an agreement to start negotiations on a verification protocol was useless and would only raise false expectations. But the United States was also committed to support and strengthen the norm established by the convention.

The big question was how the Soviet Union would react to the accusations by the United States and the proposals to strengthen the convention by most other states. Would it just deny the accusations, declare that the convention was in good shape, and claim that proposals to strengthen the convention would in fact undermine it, as it had done at the First Review Conference?

Illustrative of the change of atmosphere between the depositaries was that, in contrast with the First Review Conference, they did not introduce a joint assessment of scientific and technological developments. Instead the United States and the Soviet Union presented their own papers.[103]

The United States stressed that, although in the period since the First Review Conference no scientific break-throughs had occurred like the development of recombinant DNA techniques in the 1970s, the adaptation of these ear-lier scientific advances into widespread applications might be of even greater relevance to the convention. Whereas the possibility of using biotechnology for changing existing mi-croorganisms into biological warfare agents was played down in the joint paper submitted to the First Review Con-ference, the U.S. paper now stated that developments in this field "should be of concern" to the review conference. The possibility of genetically engineering microbial patho-gens should not be ignored, but the possibility of modifying toxins and peptides (both are biological chemicals, not bio-logical organisms) seemed to worry the United States even more. Of most concern, however, was not the potential of modified agents, but the improvements in equipment, speed, and cost of production and in creating safer condi-tions for handling biological materials. Several advances in production techniques were discussed in the U.S. paper. With these techniques, smaller equipment could produce more material in less time. As a result it had become more difficult to distinguish a large production facility from a laboratory, and the capabilities to break out of the conven-

tion in a very short time had increased. The report concluded that

> verification of the Convention, always a difficult task,
> has been significantly complicated by the new technol-
> ogy. The confidence derived from the belief that certain
> technical problems would make biological weapons un-
> attractive for the foreseeable future has eroded. The
> ease and rapidity of genetic manipulation, the ready
> availability of a variety of production equipment, the
> proliferation of safety and environmental equipment
> and health procedures to numerous laboratories and
> production facilities throughout the world, are the
> signs of the growing role of biotechnology in the world's
> economy. But these very same signs also give concern
> for the possibility of misuse of this biotechnology to
> subvert the Convention.

The document the Soviet Union submitted dealt more
in detail with the research done on many potential biological warfare agents. It discussed two new types of pathogens
in particular. But in the case both of prions (a subviral
agent that was discovered in 1982) and of AIDS, the paper's
authors concluded it unlikely that anybody would decide to
use them for warfare because the incubation period lasts
several years. The paper also noted that biotechnological
processes were not only continuously improved upon but
that the scale of biotechnological industrial processes was
increasing. An example of the former was a growth in the
efficiency of obtaining monoclonal antibodies from 1 to 2
percent to 99.5 percent. The second development—in the
scale—was illustrated by the production of recombinant human insulin. Initially 10-liter fermenters were used at high
(P3) containment level, then 150-liter fermenters were used
at P2 containment level, and now 2,000-liter fermenters
were used at P1 level.[104] The Soviet document concluded
that "the provisions of the existing Convention are broad
and universal, and therefore extend to all microorganisms

and toxins of both natural and synthetic origin which could be regarded as agents for military use."

The Reversal in the Soviet Position

The large surprise of the conference was the U-turn in the position of the Soviet Union. Until then the Soviet Union, and the other socialist states in its wake, had been very reluctant to accept any obligation to provide information or to admit foreign inspectors on its territory. But during the conference the Soviet Union suddenly emerged as a champion of strengthening the convention with a legally binding verification regime. Because the United States at the same time started opposing a verification regime, it seemed that the Soviet Union had changed positions with the United States. The reason the United States opposed a verification regime was not a fundamental aversion to intrusive verification, however, as had been the case with the Soviet Union, but a fundamental lack of trust in its feasibility.

The U.S. unwillingness to start negotiations on legally binding provisions to strengthen consultation and verification procedures did not hamper the success of the conference. Most delegations agreed that it would not be useful to start negotiations on verifying the convention as long as the conference on disarmament was still working out verification provisions of a chemical weapons convention. It was widely agreed that these provisions should serve as a model for a possible verification protocol to the Biological Weapons Convention.

The best option, therefore, seemed to be to strengthen the convention in the same manner the First Review Conference had. At that conference the final declaration had been used to record agreement on an interpretation of Article 5. This procedure was used again. But to describe the measures agreed upon at the Second Review Conference as "interpretation" or "clarification" of the convention would give a false impression of the character of these measures.

It could well be claimed that the confidence-building measures adopted in the final declaration amounted to a politically binding additional protocol to the convention.[105]

The Final Declaration

Scope

The conference confirmed that the convention unequivocally applies to "all natural or artificially created microbial or other biological agents or toxins whatever their origin or method of production."[106] To prevent any misunderstanding, it added that "consequently, toxins (both proteinaceous and non-proteinaceous) of a microbial, animal or vegetable nature and their synthetically produced analogues are covered."

Compliance

At the beginning of the conference, the U.S. delegation stated that it believed the Soviet Union had continued its offensive biological warfare program and had been involved in the production and hostile use of toxins in Laos, Cambodia, and Afghanistan. The Soviet Union strongly dismissed the accusations, but neither the United States nor the Soviet Union wanted to jeopardize the success of the conference by their argument, so the issue did not really hinder the outcome of the conference. In its final declaration, the conference simply noted statements that compliance was "subject to grave doubt in some cases and that efforts to resolve those concerns had not been successful" and noted other statements "that such a doubt was unfounded."

Declaration of Nonpossession

The convention obliges parties to destroy, or to divert to peaceful purposes, their stocks of biological and toxin weapons but does not require them to declare whether they had any weapons to eliminate.[107] The First Review Conference agreed that such declarations would help build confidence and invited parties that had not yet done so to declare that they do not possess and never have possessed such weapons, or that having possessed them they destroyed them or diverted them to peaceful purposes. The Second Review Conference, on this point at least, did not go as far as its predecessor. It only welcomed the statements made by states that had become party to the convention since the First Review Conference that they do not possess biological or toxin weapons and said "that such statements enhance confidence in the Convention." Probably one or more of these states did not like to be reminded of the biological weapons in their past.[108]

Prohibition of Transfer

Under Article 3 of the convention, parties undertook not to transfer biological and toxin weapons "to any recipient whatsoever, directly or indirectly, and not in any way to assist, encourage, or induce any State, group of States or international organizations to manufacture or otherwise acquire" such weapons. Although assistance to a terrorist organization would doubtless be a violation of both letter and spirit of the convention, the second part of Article 3 does not explicitly say so. The review conference therefore affirmed that Article 3 covers "any recipient whatsoever at international, national or sub-national levels."[109]

National Implementation Measures

The First Review Conference invited parties to provide the United Nations Center for Disarmament, for the purposes of consultation, with the texts of laws or regulations parties might have introduced to implement the convention.[110] The Second Review Conference repeated this request.[111] In addition, the conference suggested the following types of national measures that states might take to strengthen the convention's effectiveness:[112]

- Legislative, administrative, and other measures to guarantee compliance within the territory of a party
- Legislation to prevent unauthorized removal of pathogenic or toxic material
- Attention for prohibition of biological and toxin weapons in medical, scientific, and military education.

Cooperation

The issues of Sverdlovsk and yellow rain had proven that full cooperation is essential for a satisfying solution of compliance issues. The conference stressed the need "to deal seriously with compliance issues" and emphasized "that the failure to do so undermines the Convention and the arms control process in general."[113] It further appealed to parties "to make all possible efforts to solve any problems."[114]

Consultation

The First Review Conference had done little more than interpret Article 5 of the convention by making clear that consultation procedures include "the rights of any State Party subsequently to request that a consultative meeting open to all States Parties be convened at expert level."[115] The declaration did not make clear whether such a request should always be honored. The Second Review Conference went much further by agreeing "that a consultative meeting shall be promptly convened when requested by a State Party." Such a consultative meeting might consider "any problems which may arise in relation to the objective of, or in the application of the provisions of, the Convention." This, at least in theory, opened the possibility that consultative meetings would be convened at regular intervals, for instance once a year, to review scientific and technological developments and the implementation of the agreed-upon confidence-building measures.

Verification – from Article 6 to Article 5

The convention bestowed in Article 6 the right to initiate an investigation to the Security Council. The review conference, however, made use of the vague wording in Article 5 to give a consultative meeting a similar right.[116] The conference agreed that under Article 5 a consultative meeting may "suggest ways and means" to clarify ambiguous or unresolved matters and "initiate appropriate international procedures within the framework of the United Nations and in accordance with its Charter."[117] Although the conference refrained from mentioning the secretary general explicitly, the option to "initiate appropriate international procedures" can be interpreted as giving the consultative meeting the power to request the UN secretary general to investigate a possible violation of the convention. Earlier the General Assembly had opened the possibility that the secretary general would investigate accusations of use of biological weapons. Now the Security Council could also be avoided in case a party was suspected of developing, producing, or stockpiling these weapons. But it was not clear how the consultative meeting would make its decisions. If the initiation of an investigation would have to be decided by consensus, the veto power would in fact have proliferated to all parties.

Confidence-Building Measures

The main accomplishment of the Second Review Conference was probably the agreement to implement the following measures:

- Exchange of data on laboratories "that meet very high national or international safety standards"
- Exchange of data on laboratories that "specialize in permitted biological activities directly related to the Convention"
- Exchange of information on "all outbreaks of infec-

tious diseases and similar occurrences caused by toxins that seem to deviate from the normal pattern"

• Encouragement of publication of results of biological research "directly related to the Convention"

• Promotion of contacts between scientists engaged in biological research directly related to the convention.[118]

The modalities of these measures were finalized in April 1987 by a meeting of experts and are discussed in the next chapter.

Investigation of Complaints

Article 6 of the convention was envisaged to provide the procedures for handling complaints and initiating investigations. But the central role of the Security Council in this article leaves little room for new approaches, and thus the review conference built its new measures on the basis of Article 5.

An Effective Prohibition of Chemical Weapons

In Article 9 of the convention, parties pledged to "continue negotiations in good faith with a view to reaching early agreement" on an effective ban of chemical weapons. The article of the final declaration devoted to this subject performs a balancing act between noting "with satisfaction the substantial progress made in the negotiations" and "deeply" regretting that an agreement had not yet been reached.

Proliferation and International Cooperation

A close reading of Article 10 of the convention illustrates the inherent tension between the obligation not to assist in the production of biological weapons (Art. 3) and the demand that parties not be hampered in using relevant agents and technology for peaceful purposes.

The first paragraph of Article 10 lays down the right of parties to participate in "the fullest possible exchange of equipment, materials and scientific and technological information for the use of bacteriological (biological) agents and toxins for peaceful purposes" and stipulates that parties "in a position to do so" shall cooperate in contributing to the development and application of biotechnology for peaceful purposes. The second paragraph stipulates that the convention should be implemented "in a manner designed to avoid hampering . . . the international exchange of bacteriological (biological) agents and toxins and equipment for the processing, use or production of bacteriological (biological) agents and toxins for peaceful purposes. . . . "

A comparison of the two paragraphs shows that the first paragraph does not explicitly give parties the right to participate in the exchange of biological agents and toxins or in the exchange of equipment and technology for the processing and production of these agents. The second paragraph stipulates only that hampering such exchange be avoided. The paragraph reflects the need to maintain the option of controlling such exchange to prevent proliferation of biological weapons.

The convention does not make any distinction between developed and developing countries. The First Review Conference noted, however, the principle that disarmament should "help promote economic and social development, particularly in the developing countries."[119] Accordingly, it called upon parties, "especially developed countries," to increase their cooperation in the peaceful uses of the agents "particularly with developing countries." Such cooperation should include "the transfer and exchange of information, training of personnel and transfer of materials and equipment on a more systematic and long-term basis."

The final declaration of the Second Review Conference went even further in changing Article 10's emphasis. The convention had acknowledged that its implementation would not automatically further peaceful use of relevant agents (and might even hinder it) by maintaining a certain balance between a positively worded first paragraph and a more reserved second paragraph. Article 10 of the final declaration of the Second Review Conference did not reflect this balance; it only elaborated upon the first paragraph of Article 10. The paragraph of the final declaration that comes nearest to the second paragraph of Article 10 in noting the need "to avoid hampering" technological development and international cooperation in peaceful biological activities is not in Article 10 but in Article 3; the paragraph notes that measures to prevent proliferation of biological weapons "should not be used to impose restrictions" on transfer for peaceful purposes.[120]

The Second Review Conference extensively built upon the first paragraph of Article 10 of the convention. It emphasized "the increasing importance" of this article in the light of the development of biotechnology and noted "with concern the increasing gap between the developed and the developing countries" in this field. The conference accordingly urged parties to "take specific measures within their competence for the promotion of the fullest possible international co-operation in this field through their active intervention" and mentioned several such measures. The conference further recommended that measures to ensure such cooperation be pursued "within the existing means of the United Nations system." Accordingly the conference requested the secretary general "to propose for inclusion on the agenda of a relevant United Nations body a discussion and examination of the means for improving institutional mechanisms in order to facilitate the fullest possible exchange of equipment, materials and scientific and technological information for the use of bacteriological (biological) agents and toxins for peaceful purposes."[121]

This last paragraph is noteworthy because, appearance to the contrary notwithstanding, it recognizes that promoting biotechnological cooperation for peaceful purposes falls outside the scope of the review conference.[122] But the main question is whether the elaborate recommendations in Article 10 have led to concrete and substantial results, and the answer seems to be no. The recommendations have served only as a formal recognition of the preoccupations of developing countries at the review conference.

The Third Review Conference

The conference decided that a Third Review Conference would be held "at the request of a majority of States Parties not later than 1991."[123] Although the Second Review Conference had more reason to do so, it did not follow the example of the First Review Conference of congratulating itself with its spirit of cooperation. Instead, "noting the differing views with regard to verification," it decided that the Third Review Conference should inter alia consider

- the impact of scientific and technological developments
- the relevance of the results achieved in the chemical weapons negotiations
- the effectiveness of Article 5 and of the cooperative measures agreed in the final declaration
- the need for additional cooperative measures or "legally binding improvements to the Convention"—or a combination of both.

In extensively elaborating and building upon the text of the convention in a selective manner, the review conference came as close to amending the convention as a review conference could. The agreement to exchange information on certain types of laboratories and on unusual outbreaks of diseases, in particular, went much further than a review and, in fact, amounted to an agreement additional to the convention. This agreement is politically binding, not only for the parties that participated at the review conference but also for the parties that decided not to take part— certainly if they did not voice any objections when they were informed about the results of the review conference.

The Ad Hoc Meeting of Experts

From March 31 to April 15, 1987, diplomats and scientific and technical experts met in Geneva to finalize the agreed-upon measures for exchanging information. The meeting finalized the measures by elaborating them, sometimes by narrowing their scope or adding new suggestions.[124] It also drafted forms for the exchange of information, thus giving parties a standardized procedure. Seven parties presented information on relevant national institutes and activities as examples of the information parties should be giving.[125] The most important part of the meeting's report, the "Modalities for the Exchange of Information," is included in this book as appendix E.[126] Because these measures were the first worldwide confidence-building measures and because they will be reviewed and possibly augmented at the review conference in 1991, they are discussed and analyzed here in detail.

Research Centers and Laboratories

The review conference agreed on the exchange of data on laboratories that (1) meet very high national or international safety standards established for handling, for permitted purposes, biological materials that pose a high individual and community risk or (2) specialize in permitted biological activities directly related to the convention.

In specifying these measures, the ad hoc meeting narrowed their scope. Meeting "very high national *or* international safety standards" [emphasis added] was specified as having "maximum containment unit[s]." Maximum containment, in its turn, was defined by the international criteria for a "maximum containment laboratory" as specified in the World Health Organization (WHO) *Laboratory Biosafety Manual*. Laboratories that meet very high national safety standards but do not meet all the WHO criteria for a maximum containment laboratory are therefore excluded from the scope of the data exchange, even though they were included in the final declaration of the review conference. The exclusion was made because it was considered important to have a clear common understanding of what every party was supposed to declare. Several delegations, among others the Netherlands delegation, argued for agreement on a wider scope (for example, by including all facilities with high [BL3 or P3] containment). The U.S. delegation, however, felt that this would widen the scope so much that the measures would become much more difficult to implement. The U.S. delegation suggested that the exchange of data start modestly and possibly be expanded later. The narrow scope was adopted, but the meeting encouraged parties "to provide any additional information which they might consider useful to prevent or reduce the occurrence of ambiguities."[127]

The scope of the second part of this information measure also was reduced. The scope agreed upon at the review conference encompassed all "research centres and laboratories that . . . specialize in permitted biological activities directly related to the Convention." But in the report of the meeting of experts, the scope was limited to "each research centre or laboratory . . . which *has containment unit(s)* and specializes in research or development for prophylactic or protective purposes against possible hostile use of microbial and/or other biological agents or toxins" [emphasis added]. The meeting of experts did not specify what was meant by the phrase "has containment unit[s]." Whereas some parties understood this to include laboratories with BL2/P2 containment facilities, others consider only laboratories with BL3/P3 and BL4/P4 to be covered. The largest common denominator is, therefore, that laboratories that specialize in protection against biological weapons but have no or only limited containment facilities do not have to be declared. This probably excludes many smaller, but relevant, defense-oriented laboratories.[128]

The meeting also defined "permitted biological activities directly related to the Convention" as meaning "research or development for prophylactic or protective purposes against possible hostile use of microbial and/or other biological agents or toxins." I return to this definition later.

Unusual Outbreaks of Diseases

Effectively implementing the information exchange requires that parties have a common understanding of what they are expected to report. To arrive at such a common understanding was particularly difficult for the second agreed-upon measure:

> Exchange of information on all outbreaks of infectious diseases and similar occurrences caused by toxins that seem to deviate from the normal pattern as regards type, development, place, or time of occurrence. If possible, the information provided would include, as soon as it is available, data on the type of disease, approximate area affected, and number of cases.

Two concepts required clarification. What is an "outbreak," and what constitutes a "deviation from the normal pattern"? With the help of an expert of the World Health Organization, it was suggested that an outbreak be defined as

> the occurrence of an unusually large or unexpected number of cases of an illness or health-related event in a given place at a given time. The number of cases considered as unusual will vary according to the illness or event and the community concerned.[129]

It was noted, for example, that two cases associated in time and place may be sufficient to be considered an epidemic. (WHO considered the terms "outbreak" and "epidemic" interchangeable.) But no universal standards existed for "a deviation from the normal pattern." The meeting tried to remedy this by two complementary approaches:

1. Parties were encouraged "to fully utilize existing reporting systems within the WHO" and to provide background information on the "normal" occurrence of diseases caused by organisms in risk groups 3 and 4.[130] This background of normal outbreaks would help other parties to understand ambiguous reports on unusual outbreaks as normal.

2. A number of cases were mentioned in which exchange of data on unusual outbreaks was considered partic-

ularly important. (It is remarkable that, although the review conference agreed that all abnormal outbreaks should be reported, by giving a list of cases in which exchange of data was considered "particularly important" the group seemed to admit that some abnormal outbreaks should be considered more abnormal than others.)

Reports should be given "promptly after cognizance of the outbreak," and parties were encouraged (1) to invite experts from other parties to help handle an outbreak and (2) to respond favorably to such invitations. Finally, a link was provided with the authority of the secretary general to investigate information concerning possible use of biological weapons. The meeting explicitly drew attention to the possibility that the secretary general of the United Nations might be requested to investigate outbreaks "that could be interpreted as resulting from the use of bacteriological (biological) or toxin weapons."[131]

Encouragement to Publish

The third confidence-building measure reads as follows:

> Encouragement of publication of results of biological research directly related to the Convention, in scientific journals generally available to States Parties, as well as promotion of use for permitted purposes of knowledge gained in this research.

The meeting had to address two problems: how to publish the results of scientific research often complicated by national security or commercial interests and how to define "research directly related to the Convention." Research for prophylactic and protective purposes, for example, is to a large extent based on an assessment of the biological weapon threat of potential adversaries. Publishing all the details of this research might give an accurate picture of such an assessment and thus help a country preparing to use biological weapons offensively estimate the effect of different types of biological warfare and adjust its production and employment plans accordingly. A lot of research, furthermore, is directed at developing new commercial products, such as pharmaceutics. Complete openness of this often very expensive research might give the results of one company's investments to other companies for free.

As a compromise solution, the meeting recommended that "basic research in biosciences, and particularly that directly related to the Convention should generally be unclassified," and "applied research to the extent possible, without infringing on national and commercial interests, should also be unclassified." Both parts of this paragraph are full of qualifications, the second part even more so than the first part.[132] The paragraph therefore does not amount to much more than an encouragement of openness of research.

For this measure the meeting did not clarify the meaning of "research directly related to the Convention." This lack of definition is in contrast with the first confidence-building measure. There the meeting agreed to specify the object of data exchange on "laboratories that . . . specialize in permitted biological activities directly related to the Convention" as a laboratory "which has containment unit[s] and specializes in research or development for prophylactic or protective purposes against possible hostile use of microbial and/or other biological agents or toxins." One would expect that the meeting would have defined the phrase "directly related to the Convention" as meaning "for prophylactic or protective purposes." The meeting thought, however, that a somewhat wider scope would be preferable but was not able to agree on a clear description. It did specifically draw attention to publication of research carried out in the laboratories that had to be declared under the first measure and research on outbreaks of diseases covered by the second measure.

Failing to define the scope might encourage parties to provide information on all publications regarding research of infectious diseases. The number of such articles is often so large that exchange of the titles would overwhelm the exchange system. Most of these articles are of very little relevance for the BWC, and on top of that, they are usually well publicized in specialist publications that are generally available. The meeting therefore encouraged parties to provide information on the generally available scientific publications in which research results are published.[133]

The meeting also supported international cooperation in the safe handling of biological material covered by the convention.[134] Such cooperation would help to build confidence that the biological materials and the locations where they are handled are not misused for development, production, or storage of biological weapons. It is, after all, improbable that a country would admit foreigners to a facility where it is violating the convention.

Active Promotion of Contacts

The last of the four measures agreed to at the review conference was the following:

> Active promotion of contacts between scientists engaged in biological research directly related to the Convention, including exchanges for joint research on a mutually agreed basis.

In elaborating the measure, the meeting encouraged parties "to the extent possible" to give information

> • on planned international conferences, seminars, symposia and similar events dealing with biological research directly related to the Convention
> • on other opportunities for exchange of scientists, joint research or other measures to promote contacts between scientists engaged in biological research directly related to the Convention.

The idea behind this measure is that professional contacts, joint research projects, and similar activities will prevent or reduce doubts about the activities of the scientists and institutes involved. A concrete example of such international contacts is the encouragement by the meeting to invite experts from other parties to help handle an outbreak of infectious diseases and similar occurrences caused by toxins and to respond favorably to such invitations.[135]

Procedures

The meeting agreed that all the information should be

- provided in one of the official languages of the convention (English, Russian, French, Spanish, or Chinese)
- sent to the UN Department for Disarmament Affairs
- promptly forwarded, in the form received, to all states parties
- also made available to the World Health Organization.

Information "to be given on an annual basis" should be provided no later than April 15 and should cover the previous calendar year. This concerns mainly the data exchange on laboratories and the follow-up on reports of unusual outbreaks of diseases. The first report on such an abnormal outbreak should "be given promptly after cognizance of the outbreak" and certainly not saved for the yearly information exchange.[136] Publication of the results of research should of course take place throughout the year, but lists of particularly relevant articles and publications could be given or updated annually. Information on opportunities for international scientific contacts should obviously be given as soon as available.

Consultation and Verification

The so-called meeting of scientific and technical experts did much more than elaborate the technicalities of the mea-

sures agreed on at the review conference and was in many
respects more a political than a technical meeting. This is
evident from the measures discussed above and also from
the following text:[137]

> The *experts* note that, should any *question* arise in
> relation to the objective of, or in the application of the
> provisions of, the Convention, including as regards the
> information and data which States Parties have under-
> taken to exchange, States Parties can make use of the
> provisions for consultation and co-operation under Ar-
> ticle V of the Convention. . . . [Emphasis added.]

Now this is less self-evident than it may seem. The convention provides for consultations to consider "problems which
may arise in relation to the objective of, or in the application of the provisions of, the Convention," but no mention is
made of problems, let alone questions, regarding the provisions of the final declaration of a review conference. It is
questionable whether this enlargement of the role of consultative meetings actually fell within the mandate of the
meeting, and that probably explains why this part of the
report was attributed to the experts specifically. This
choice of words could be interpreted to mean the following:
You asked the ad hoc meeting to finalize the modalities of
the exchange of information, but we, the experts, like to
add that in our view

• the information that parties have undertaken to exchange is subject to Article 5 of the convention (which implies that it can be put on the agenda of consultative meetings), and

• these consultative meetings could consider "questions," although the convention and the final declaration of
the two review conferences speak only about "problems."
(The first word does not imply doubts and suspicions like
the latter.)

Up until the summer of 1990, a consultative meeting had never been convened. But if it were, this part of the agreed modalities would open the possibility for the parties to inquire, for example, about laboratories that other parties have, or should have, declared, not only in case they suspected a violation, but just as a matter of routine.

Costs

In retrospect the meeting of experts seems to have been more interested in elaborating the good intentions of the Second Review Conference than in working out all the practical details of the measures, because the costs of implementation, a very mundane but crucial aspect, was largely overlooked. The only mention of costs in the report of the meeting is a footnote in which it is noted that the secretary general considered that

> he would be required to render technical services and assistance . . . , it being understood that such services and assistance would have no financial implications for the regular budget of the United Nations and that all related costs would be met by the States Parties to the Convention in accordance with the rules of procedure adopted by the Second Review Conference.[138]

To limit costs, the meeting agreed that the UN Department for Disarmament Affairs would forward the provided information in the form received (thereby limiting the readability and accessibility of the information).

Additional Considerations

Finally, the meeting's report mentioned proposals that were considered but not adopted. The meeting suggested that the Third Review Conference would take note of these proposals.[139] The meeting explicitly encouraged parties in the meantime to provide any additional information they might consider useful to prevent doubts and suspicions.

Revalidation and Proliferation, 1986–1990

If the convention was critically ill in 1986, it has certainly recovered somewhat since then. The main cause for this recovery was without doubt the radical improvement of the East-West climate. The modest confidence-building measures that were agreed upon at the Second Review Conference also have played a role, be it more the role of revalidation exercises than of a miracle drug. The data provided by parties, and the increased contacts at international conferences, have built some confidence, even if so far only about a quarter of all parties have participated in the exchange of information.

A North-South Problem?

Arms control and disarmament negotiations were considered for a long time as primarily a matter between East and West. Almost the only neutral and nonaligned countries that played an active role in these negotiations were neutrals (such as Sweden) and nonaligned countries (such as Yugoslavia) geographically located directly between East and West. The Biological Weapons Convention was not an exception to this. The negotiations on the BWC and at both review conferences were mainly conducted by the countries of the East and West and Sweden. Even the possible use of toxin weapons in Afghanistan and Southeast Asia was much more an issue between East and West, and especially between the United States and the Soviet Union, than an issue for the countries in the region. All this has changed. Although the United States remains seriously concerned about a biological weapons program of the Soviet Union, the relations between East and West have greatly improved, and the concerns about the proliferation and use of weapons of mass destruction in the developing world have grown into one of the highest priorities on the arms control agenda.

Signs of Proliferation

During the last months of 1988 and the beginning of 1989 several reports surfaced about countries that seemed interested in acquiring biological weapons.

North Korea, Iran, and Iraq are among the countries mentioned. North Korea was said to be cooperating with Syria in the development of biological weapons and to have had a capability for using biological weapons offensively since the early 1980s.[140] In 1988 the U.S. Department of Defense stated that 10 countries possessed biological weapons.[141] According to an Iraqi army document gained by the *Observer*, Iraqi army units were required to take stock of all chemical and biological weapons at the disposal of the unit.[142] In January 1989 Iraq was said to be experimenting with biological weapons in at least four locations.[143] It had acquired small quantities of mycotoxins from a company in West Germany.[144] The quantities were of no military relevance, but they had no known civil application and therefore might indicate that Iraq was involved in research of biological weapons. According to another report, Iraq had acquired tularemia out of the United States.[145] The United States had used tularemia to fill biological weapons. In September 1990 U.S. intelligence sources disclosed that Iraq would be able to use significant quantities of deadly biological agents, including anthrax, on the battlefield by early 1991.[146] In November 1990 Yasir Arafat, the chairman of the Palestine Liberation Organization, was reported to have said, after meeting with the Iraqi president earlier in the week, that in case of war Iraq would use anthrax.[147] The threat of use of biological weapons was considered to be so serious that U.S. and British forces in the Gulf area were immunized against anthrax.

In 1987 the United States is said to have learned of

Iranian efforts to develop biological weapons from documents on board an Iranian ship that was caught laying mines in the Gulf.[148] Speaking at a seminar organized for the ground forces commanders in October 1988, Ali Akbar Hashemi-Rafsanjani, at that time acting commander in chief of the Iranian armed forces, was reported to have said, "Chemical and biological weapons are [a] poor man's atomic bombs and can easily be produced. We should at least consider them for our defense."[149] On January 18, 1989, the U.S. network ABC News reported that Iran had been trying for at least two years to develop biological weapons but so far had not succeeded.[150] The news report quoted unidentified U.S. intelligence sources as saying that Iran used several front companies to try to buy equipment such as 1,000-liter fermenters to grow large quantities of organisms and safety equipment to deal with dangerous agents. These front companies were under orders of a part of the Revolutionary Guards responsible for weapons development. As far as the quoted sources knew, the efforts to buy such equipment had not been successful.

Reactions

The production and subsequent use of chemical weapons by Iraq offers some important lessons. Iraq secretly built production plants for chemical weapons, importing most of the necessary technology and materials from the West. Iraq subsequently proved willing to use chemical weapons in flagrant violation of the Geneva Protocol (of which it was a party). The Western industrialized countries now knew that some countries were willing to violate their treaty obligations and that the Western countries themselves might unwillingly get involved because the technology and materials needed for the violation would be imported from them. The signs that a few countries were actively trying to acquire a biological warfare capability therefore worried them. But what to do?

The production of the most deadly chemical weapons

requires large quantities of precursor chemicals that are produced by a few companies worldwide for a limited number of civil applications. This opened the possibility of export controls for these chemicals. Export of (usually small) quantities for civil purposes could be approved, whereas export of large quantities for dubious purposes could be prevented. The export control measures taken were not perfect, but as an interim measure in anticipation of a chemical weapons convention, they have helped.

The situation with biological weapons was much more complicated. Biological agents reproduce themselves, and the same is true for the organisms that produce toxins. So, in contrast with chemical weapons, no large quantities of precursors are needed. A country that wants to produce biological weapons will probably try to acquire (1) strains of the organisms (small quantities sufficient); (2) equipment and materials for large-scale reproduction such as fermenters, cultivating agents, and harvesters; (3) equipment for handling hazardous materials; and (4) equipment for conserving and disseminating agents. The problem is that most of this is also needed for such peaceful purposes as the production of vaccines. The techniques used for producing a vaccine against a disease and for producing a warfare agent to disseminate the same disease are strikingly similar. In both cases the organism that causes the disease is reproduced in large quantities. In the case of vaccine production, however, the disease-causing organism is either changed or killed to prevent it from causing the disease.

Efforts to stem the proliferation of biological weapons are severely hindered by the fact that the technology needed for the production of biological weapons is largely identical with the technology needed for medical care and veterinary medicine. A policy of denying countries such technology would be unacceptable both from a humanitarian and a political point of view and, certainly in the long run, impossible to implement. The only way to prevent the proliferation of biological weapons is to strengthen the BWC.

That is not to say that in the meantime nothing could or should be done to prevent countries from producing or using biological weapons. The least governments are obliged to do is to warn relevant research establishments and companies in their countries against the danger that they might unwittingly get involved in the production of biological weapons. Many countries have given out such warnings. In addition particular relevant items, such as equipment for cultivating, harvesting, and conserving biological organisms, could be brought under export controls. But as such controls can hurt bona fide trade, the civil relevance of international trade in the item will have to be weighed against the risk of it being used to acquire biological weapons.

Two Cases

In December 1988 an Iranian pharmacologist named Moallam asked Dr. Bruno Schiefer, the director of the toxicology research center of the University of Saskatchewan (Canada) where he could possibly obtain cultures of two types of T-2 trichothecene mycotoxin producing fungal strains.[151] The toxins produced by these kinds of cultures were much talked about as the possible active ingredients of yellow rain. In theory these fungal cultures can be found in nature, but in practice this is very difficult. The fungal cultures concerned had been sought for years by Western scientists. Dr. Schiefer found the request unusual and informed the Canadian government. In accordance with the informal procedures established between the members of the Australian group, other governments were informed.[152] Upon receiving the information, the Netherlands government immediately contacted the Centraal Bureau voor Schimmelculturen (Central Bureau for Fungal Cultures) in Baarn.[153] A few days later the bureau received a letter from the "Iranian Research Organization for Science & Technology" asking for 11 different mycotoxins producing fungal cultures. Except for research no civil uses were known of these cultures and toxins.[154] The order was not accepted, and the other members of the Australian group were warned.

Alerted by the signs of proliferation, the Netherlands government, in the beginning of 1989, started warning relevant companies and institutes such as the National Institute of Public Health and Environmental Hygiene in Bilthoven.[155] This institute had an international reputation in the field of vaccine production and had helped many countries to produce their own vaccines. At the beginning of 1989 a request to train Iranians in the production of vaccines was pending.[156] This was not unusual. It could be expected that a country the size of Iran would eventually try to acquire the technology to produce some of the vaccines needed for its national health care. With a population of about 50 million, national production of vaccines would be cheaper than importing them. The statements and events described above made the Netherlands government wary, however, about getting involved in what might prove to be production of biological weapons, even though Iran was party to the Biological Weapons Convention. The National Institute (a governmental institute) therefore did not agree to the Iranian request. At the same time the Ministry for Foreign Affairs stumbled upon a related transaction that was much further advanced. Contact-Flow, a company based near Rotterdam, had for years been building fermenters for vaccine production. Orders had been coming from all over the world. Now Contact-Flow was in the process of delivering such equipment to Iran. It is a classic example of the problems involved in using export controls to prevent the production of biological weapons. Fermenters for vaccine production were not subjected to export controls, so export could be stopped only by persuading the company to discontinue the order.[157] But no proof was available that Iran would use these fermenters to produce biological weapons. Iran had a legitimate interest in producing vaccines, the fermenters were specifically designed for that purpose, and the company would have had to pay a heavy fine if it had not fulfilled the contract. The order was carried out.

2

The Current State of the Biological Weapons Convention

This chapter questions the current state of the Biological Weapons Convention from three perspectives. First, how are technological developments and new attitudes toward weapons of mass destruction affecting the threat of biological weapons? Second, what is the concept underlying the scope of the convention and what are the problems involved in this concept? Finally, what are the shortcomings of the measures produced at the two first review conferences?

A Growing Threat?

The interest in biological weapons has clearly grown since the convention came into effect in 1975. The accusations by the United States that the Soviet Union was involved in biological warfare and the Soviet Union's inadequate reaction to these accusations attracted a lot of attention and might have given the impression that biological weapons had become an interesting option to the military. This impression was reinforced by the reports that Iraq had acquired a biological weapon capability. Many scientists still doubt, however, that the developments in biotechnology have made or will make biological warfare a real military option. This chapter reviews the factors most frequently mentioned to explain the growing interest in biological weapons.[1]

Better Prophylaxis

An important reason biological weapons are not considered effective weapons is not a lack of lethal agents but a lack of measures to control the results of their use. If effective measures could be developed to protect one's own troops (and population) against the effects of biological or toxin weapons, these weapons might become more attractive.[2] No developments of such a "controllable" type of biological warfare have been reported, but it is likely that medical and pharmaceutical research will bring diseases increasingly under control. As long as the results of such research are public (and that is a strong argument for complete openness), the option of using these diseases in hostilities will not become more attractive. But biotechnology has opened the possibility of secretly and quickly producing large quantities of vaccines. Producing enough to vaccinate its own armed forces and population might make it easier for a country to prepare for offensive use of biological weapons. It is, however, very unlikely that a large-scale vaccination program would go unnoticed.

New and Improved Agents

The possibility of using advanced biotechnology to produce new diseases for use as biological warfare agents is sometimes mentioned as the most important reason for the growing interest in biological weapons. There are no concrete indications, however, of the development of new agents that are more effective than existing diseases. Certainly as far as the lethality of existing diseases is concerned, it seems very unlikely that anybody would find it useful to "improve" upon it.

Less improbable than the development of new biological agents might be attempts to improve upon the effectiveness of existing agents. Theoretically modern biotechnological methods might, for example, enhance a biological agent's resistance to degradation (as the result of sunshine, humidity, et cetera) during its dissemination or, conversely, accelerate degradation after its use.[3] Another possibility might involve altering agents to complicate detection and diagnosis or to speed infection. One of the most outspoken proponents of this theory is Dr. Erhard Geissler, who writes that "it is now conceivable that recombinant DNA research and other biotechnologies could be misused in order to design and – in violation of the BW Convention – to develop" militarily useful biological and toxin weapons.[4] No concrete evidence seems to exist that any country is actively pursuing such a goal, but it could, for example, be the spin-off of the development of biological pesticides for use in agriculture.[5]

On the other hand, it should be noted that the working group on chemical and biological weapons of the 39th Pugwash Conference (Cambridge, Massachusetts, July 23–28, 1989) concluded that

> recent alarms about genetic engineering furnishing military attractive new "designer agents" had arisen very largely out of ignorance; for as we went down the list of the particular properties that contribute to the aggressiveness of a substance and may make it seem worth weaponizing, we were not able to see how a biotechnological-process product could satisfy them any better than could toxic or infective substances already available. If anything, the new technologies seemed more likely to favour the defence than the offence – to increase the strength of protection against biological weapons rather than that of the weapons themselves.[6]

New Production Technologies

The most relevant contribution of recent biotechnological developments to the renewed interest in biological and toxin

weapons is probably the enormous progress made in reproduction technology and the proliferation of this civil technology all over the world. If production of a small quantity
of biological agents or toxins took several days 10 years
ago, a quantity of 10 to 100 times as large can now often be
produced within a few hours. Producing agents in quantities large enough for military use so quickly might make a
breakout of the convention easier.

Technologies for Storage and Dissemination

An existing method to protect biological agents during
dissemination is microencapsulation. This technique of
coating microorganisms or toxins is being developed for
civil use (to protect microorganisms during a production
process in bio-reactors or to protect microbial pesticides
during their dissemination), but it is conceivable that it
could be applied to biological weapons purposes. Such
technologies also might make it easier to store biological
weapons.

Application as Weapons of Terror

Biological weapons continue to be considered ineffective
weapons for tactical warfare. If the purpose of their use is
to terrorize civilians, however, some might consider them an
alternative to chemical weapons or conventional missiles.
Examples that come to mind are the bombing of Halabja
with chemical weapons and the Iraqi missile attacks
against Israel and Saudi Arabia. Animal and plant diseases
could possibly be used for "economic war fighting." These
applications are not new, but interest in them might be
growing.

The possibility that biological weapons might be used
by terrorists is often mentioned, but there are very few
reports that any terrorist group has ever tried or threatened
to use them.[7]

Conclusion

Since the Biological Weapons Convention came into force, the fear that biological weapons might be used has not vanished; instead, it has revived. This fear has been spurred by the interest some regimes have shown in acquiring biological weapons probably for terrorizing external and internal adversaries. Fears about use also have been heightened by the development and worldwide spread of civil biotechnology that allows large quantities of biological agents to be produced quickly.

The risk that biotechnology's fast development will result in more effective biological warfare agents and therefore make biological weapons more attractive for tactical combat cannot be discarded. But at least for the foreseeable future, this risk does not seem very large. The current interest in biological weapons shown by some countries seems to be directed solely at acquiring existing biological and toxin agents.

The Underlying Concept

This concept underlies the Biological Weapons Convention: effective prevention of biological warfare requires prohibiting not only use itself but also, as far as possible, the route to such use. The most important difference between the Geneva Protocol and the BWC, therefore, is the scope of the activities these treaties cover. Because the Geneva Protocol ban on the use of chemical and biological weapons did not give sufficient confidence that these weapons would not be used, the 1972 Biological Weapons Convention complemented the Geneva Protocol with a ban on the most important activities that precede any use of biological weapons—that is, the development, production, and stockpiling of these weapons. Not all steps on the route to the use of biological weapons, however, were covered by the convention.

A country that wants to use biological weapons not only has to acquire biological warfare agents, but it also has to develop an effective weapon and to introduce that weapon with its armed forces. It is important to distinguish these phases: acquiring a capability to produce biological warfare agents is absolutely not identical to acquiring a capability to use biological weapons.

The following list indicates the progression of steps a country has to take to produce chemical and biological warfare agents. This comparison between chemical and biological warfare agents illustrates the typical properties of biological warfare agents.

	Chemical Weapons	*Biological Weapons*
1.	fundamental research	fundamental research
	↓	↓
2.	applied research	applied research
	↓	↓
3.	development	development[8]
	↓	↓
4.	open-air testing	open-air testing
	↓	↓
5.	development of production process	development of production process
	↓	↓
6.	small-scale production at pilot plant	small-scale production at pilot plant
	↓	↓
7.	production of precursors	—
	↓	↓
8.	building of production installation	—
	↓	↓
9.	production of agent	production of agent
	↓	↓
10.	—	conservation of agent

The routes differ for the following reasons:

- Biological agents are produced by nature, whereas chemical agents have to be developed and produced by people out of other, so-called precursor chemicals. In theory biotechnology makes development of "improved" biological warfare agents feasible, but in practice the agents available in nature suffice.
- Biological agents reproduce themselves in the body of the victim. A minimal militarily relevant quantity is therefore several factors smaller than a minimal militarily relevant quantity of chemical weapons. Production of a militarily relevant quantity of biological warfare agents thus can take place in a pilot plant-sized facility.
- For biological weapons to be effective, the biological agents should stay alive during storage, transport, handling, firing, and impact of the weapon. This presents considerable problems.[9]

The usual route to toxin warfare agents is largely the same as the route to biological agents. They are produced by biological organisms. Although they do not reproduce in the body of the victim, their toxicity is often so high that a minimal militarily relevant quantity will still be much smaller than that of a chemical nerve agent. Some toxins can also be produced by chemical synthesis. In that case the route is of course the same as for chemical agents.

As illustrated by the list, the production of biological warfare agents does not require precursors or large-scale production equipment. The same is true for the old-fashioned way of producing toxin agents when their toxicity is very high, such as in the case of saxitoxin. Large-scale fermenters would be needed if the toxicity of the toxin were comparable to that of ordinary chemical agents. Because biological agents are living organisms, their conservation requires more attention than the conservation of chemical agents (including toxins).

Finally, it should be pointed out that a country that wishes to acquire chemical or biological warfare agents could skip these routes if it managed to import the agents.

Because the most relevant agents have no, or almost no, civil applications, importing relevant quantities is usually impossible.[10] But a country can often skip several important steps by importing relevant equipment and materials.

Acquiring a militarily relevant quantity of biological warfare agents is not easy, but it is a light task in comparison with the problems involved in turning the agents into a militarily useful weapon. It can be argued that so far nobody has succeeded in developing a militarily useful biological weapon. The following list of steps illustrates that the route from possession of warfare agents to actual use of a weapon is largely the same for biological weapons and chemical weapons. A notable difference is the immunization that is possible against most biological and toxin agents, but not against the common chemical warfare agents.

	Chemical Weapons	*Biological Weapons*
11.	development of dissemination techniques	development of dissemination techniques
	↓	↓
12.	production of dissemination equipment	production of dissemination equipment
	↓	↓
13.	filling of shells, bombs, etc.	filling of shells, bombs, etc.
	↓	↓
14.	integration into military doctrine	integration into military doctrine
	↓	↓
15.	deployment	deployment
	↓	↓
16.	training in use	training in use
	↓	↓
17.	physical protection	physical protection
	↓	↓
18.	–	prophylaxis by immunization
	↓	↓
19.	use	use

Whereas all steps leading to a stockpile of agents could in theory be skipped by import, use of the agents as weapons requires steps, such as integration into the military doctrine and training in use, that the country must take itself.

Conceptual Limitations

Many of the convention's shortcomings stem from the fact that the concept described above is fine in theory, but very difficult to implement. Most of the steps leading to the use of biological weapons can also be necessary for civil purposes; therefore, a blanket prohibition is not possible. Development and production of vaccines against a microorganism, for example, have much in common with the development and production of that microorganism as a biological warfare agent. And even if no civil applications exist, development and production of an agent might be justified by protective purposes. Table 1 illustrates which activities described above the BWC prohibits. The table makes clear that the main criterion for permission or prohibition is the purpose of a certain activity. That is why the convention in its present form is virtually unverifiable: intentions are extremely difficult to verify.

The scope, and thus the significance, of the Biological Weapons Convention is not only determined by the activities mentioned in the list but also by the agents that are covered. The convention also leaves room for question marks on this score. Agents that can cause disease in animals or plants are usually considered to be covered, but misunderstandings do arise because the convention does not mention them specifically.[11] In addition the scope of the convention excludes quantities of agents that are justified for prophylactic, protective, or other peaceful purposes, but it does not set any limit on such quantities.

Research

The Biological Weapons Convention bans development but does not mention research. But what is the difference? The

TABLE 1
Activities Permitted or Prohibited in the
Biological Weapons Convention, by Purpose

Activity	Purpose		
	Civil	Protection	Offense
1. Fundamental research	permitted	permitted	not prohibited
2. Applied research	permitted	permitted	not prohibited
3. Development	permitted	permitted	banned
4. Open-air testing	permitted	permitted	banned
5. Development of production process	permitted	permitted	not prohibited
6. Small-scale production at pilot plant	permitted	permitted	banned
7. Production of precursors	N.A.	N.A.	N.A.
8. Building of production installation	permitted	permitted	not prohibited
9. Production of agent	permitted	permitted	banned
10. Conservation of agent	permitted	permitted*	banned
11. Development of dissemination techniques	permitted	permitted*	banned
12. Production of dissemination equipment	permitted	permitted*	banned
13. Filling of shells, bombs, etc.	N.A.	N.A.	banned
14. Integration in military doctrine	N.A.	N.A.	not prohibited
15. Deployment	N.A.	N.A.	banned
16. Training in use			
with mock agents	N.A.	N.A.	not prohibited
with real agents	N.A.	N.A.	banned
17. Physical protection	N.A.	permitted	not prohibited
18. Prophylaxis by immunization	permitted	permitted	not prohibited
19. Use	N.A.	N.A.	**

*It is questionable whether these activities could be justified for protective purposes.

**The BWC does not explicitly prohibit use, but excludes its possibility.

N.A. = Not applicable.

convention makes no effort to answer that question. This
lack of clarity is dangerous, as the equipment needed for
producing biological warfare agents on a relevant scale is
not very different from the equipment used for research.

Research of biological weapons was not banned because
it was considered to be impossible to make a clear and objective distinction between research for permitted purposes
and research with the intention of producing biological warfare agents. Take, for example, research into a rare and very
virulent disease. The most obvious reason for such research
would be purely medical or scientific. Such research might,
however, be undertaken with the intent to use the disease
for biological warfare. Or a country might start research to
develop prophylactic and protective measures out of fear of
another party.[12] An independent observer would probably
not be able to tell for sure for what purpose the research
activities he observed were undertaken. It was argued that
a ban on research would therefore not lead to more confidence but instead would lead to accusations that could be
neither validated nor disproved.

But development was banned, and if this ban is to make
sense, it has to be clear to all parties which activities are to
be considered as "development," and therefore banned or
restricted, and which activities are regarded as research,
and therefore not restricted. Regrettably, as the following
comparison between "pure" research, applied research, and
development illustrates, it is very difficult to draw a clear
line between research and development.

"Pure" Research

Purpose: Systematic search for new knowledge **without**
any specific applications in mind
Methods: Theoretical studies; observation; experiments
Scale: In the case of chemical and biological research,
very small[13]

Applied Research

Purpose: Systematic search for knowledge **with** specific
applications in mind

Methods: The same as pure research
Scale: Small (for biological research)

Development

Purpose: Systematic utilization of new knowledge for specific applications
Methods: The same as research, plus tests needed for production (pilot plants) and introduction on market (testing ecological effects, etc.)
Scale: Usually larger than research, but nevertheless still quite small.

The main difference between research and development seems to be the intention with which the activities take place. But intentions cannot be verified. For all practical purposes a sliding scale exists between fundamental research and development of new warfare agents. Essentially the same methods are used, although testing production processes in a pilot plant for pure research purposes seems unlikely. And although the quantities of agents needed for research purposes will generally be smaller than those needed for development, even the scale of the activities is not really a distinguishing factor. An example of the confusion about the distinction between research and development was given by the U.S. Department of Defense in 1984 when it claimed that

> the Soviet Union has an active R&D program to investigate and evaluate the utility of biological weapons and their impact on the combat environment. The Soviet effort in biological warfare violates the Biological and Toxin Weapons Convention of 1972, which was ratified by the USSR. The convention bans the research, development, production and possession of biological agents and toxins for warfare purposes.[14]

The main mistake made here is that the convention does not ban research. One could argue that research "for warfare purposes" would be against the spirit of the convention, but research "to investigate and evaluate the utility of biological weapons and their impact on the combat environment" could be undertaken for protective purposes and would not be a violation.

A solution could be found by explicitly prohibiting offensive research. But quantitative constraints on research and development for protective purposes and, above all, complete openness of all such research would probably be more effective.

Testing

Testing of chemical or biological weapons is not explicitly forbidden but would fall under the ban on development. But testing for purposes of protection and prophylaxis is not forbidden; neither is research on the dissemination of microorganisms. An outside observer might find it difficult to determine the purpose of certain tests.

The solution should probably be sought in constraints on the allowed tests (for example, a prohibition on all open-air tests with real agents and an obligation to declare tests with simulants and invite foreign observers) and, again above all, in complete openness.

Preparations for Use

The Biological Weapons Convention does not explicitly prohibit preparations for use of biological weapons such as integrating biological warfare into the military doctrine and training in the use of biological weapons (as long as no real agents are used for that purpose). The relevance of integrating these weapons into military plans and doctrine and of training in their use is sometimes underestimated: if a country acquires biological or chemical warfare agents, it cannot immediately use them effectively. Experience shows that the effect of chemical and biological weapons usually has been severely limited because the commanders did not really know what to do with them and the soldiers were not well prepared.

Explicitly prohibiting preparations for the use of biological weapons would therefore be useful, even though such prohibition would be difficult to verify. Training to use biological or chemical weapons is in many respects identical with (permitted) training for protection against these weapons. But that is no reason to allow countries to prepare for offensive biological warfare. If it became clear that a party to the convention was training its commanders and troops to use biological weapons, it is improbable that other parties would consider this legitimate behavior, even if no indication existed that biological weapons were being produced. For similar reasons Sweden has proposed that the chemical weapons convention prohibit preparations for use of chemical weapons. So far no consensus has been reached on this proposal.[15]

Protection and Prophylaxis

Protection and prophylaxis are permitted by both conventions because biological and chemical weapons are not very effective against well-protected soldiers. Retaining protective equipment will therefore make it easier for countries to forgo the option of retaliation in kind and become party to the convention. It will also discourage violations. But retaining effective protective and prophylactic equipment is difficult without testing them with real agents. Development and production for these purposes is therefore permitted, whereas development and production "of types and in quantities that have no justification for prophylactic, protective or other peaceful purposes" is forbidden. But what is the difference? What types and quantities "have no justification for prophylactic, protective, or other peaceful purposes"? Clear and generally accepted answers to these questions do not exist. As development for protective purposes is often kept confidential, doubts about the real purpose of activities in this field can easily come up.

Use

The chemical weapons convention will prohibit the use of chemical weapons. The text of the Biological Weapons Convention does not prohibit the use of biological and toxin weapons, but the absolute prohibition to "stockpile or otherwise acquire or retain" these weapons clearly implies the prohibition of their use.

Toxins

The convention covers toxins, whatever their origin or method of production. This leaves no doubt that every toxin is covered, but nevertheless the Second Review Conference considered it wise to declare that "toxins (both proteinaceous and non-proteinaceous) of a microbial, animal or vegetable nature and their synthetically produced analogues are covered."[16] The purpose of this declaration was not primarily to reaffirm that all toxins were covered (the convention is clear enough) but to come to a clearer understanding about which chemicals should be considered toxins. The Second Review Conference has contributed to this purpose, but it seems probable that, as technology develops, the distinction between toxins and synthetically produced chemicals will become blurred even more. A chemical weapons convention might eventually obviate the necessity to refine the definition of toxins.

Animal and Plant Diseases

Article 1 of the convention prohibits developing, producing, acquiring, and retaining biological agents or toxins "of types and in quantities that have no justification for prophylactic, protective, or other peaceful purposes." This leaves no room to doubt that its scope also encompasses hostile use of biological agents or toxins against animals or plants. It is nevertheless remarkable that neither the convention nor the final declarations of the review conferences specifically mention hostile use of biological agents or toxins that can cause disease in animals or plants. In the negotiations on a chemical weapons ban, animals have been included in the definition of toxic chemical, but herbicides are excluded.[17] To prevent any misunderstanding, the hostile use of biological agents should be placed explicitly within the scope of the convention.

Exceptions

By implication, Article 1 of the convention excludes from its scope biological agents and toxins of types and in quantities that are justified for prophylactic, protective, or other peaceful purposes. But which types and quantities are justified?

For prophylactic and protective purposes production and stockpiling of all types of potential biological and toxin warfare agents could apparently be justified. But what quantities are justified for such purposes? A party might argue that large quantities are needed to test protection equipment and to produce vaccines. Production of large quantities of exotic diseases for such purposes might give rise, however, to suspicions about the party's real intentions.

And what about use of biological agents for domestic law enforcement? In the convention's preamble the parties express their determination "to exclude completely the possibility of bacteriological (biological) agents and toxins being used as weapons." This argues for a prohibition of use for law enforcement. But the Geneva Protocol does not prohibit such use, and law enforcement is often considered to be a peaceful purpose, so it could be argued that the convention allows production and stockpiling of biological and toxin agents for law enforcement purposes.[18] Accepting the latter argument causes trouble because of the large gray area between domestic law enforcement and internal conflict. If biological agents could be used against hijackers of an airplane, would they also be allowed against terrorists occupying a building or against rebels who have taken over a village?

The negotiators on a Chemical Weapons Convention (CWC) are wrestling with a similar problem. For the sake of clarity, they have excluded law enforcement from the list of permitted peaceful purposes.[19] But it is still included in the definition of "purposes not prohibited under the convention."[20] Even so, the rolling text – that is, the draft convention that is periodically revised – contains a phrase within brackets indicating that no provisional agreement has been reached on the text and implying that the use of a chemical for domestic law enforcement and riot control is allowed only if the chemical is not lethal and if its use for such purposes is approved by the Conference of States Parties.[21] It seems advisable to leave no doubt that any use of biological agents for law enforcement is prohibited.

Shortcomings of the Confidence-Building Measures

The confidence-building measures agreed upon by the Second Review Conference restored some confidence in the convention, but they require improvement in many respects. The Stockholm International Peace Research Institute (SIPRI) has published a detailed evaluation of the measures and their implementation.[22] This discussion is limited to the main shortcomings.

Participation

The Second Review Conference urged parties "to promptly apply these measures and report the data agreed upon" pending the results of the meeting of experts. In fact, however, not a single country reported any data to the UN Department for Disarmament Affairs before the meeting of experts convened in Geneva on March 31, 1987.[23] During the meeting seven countries reported relevant data, and by July 1990 the number of participating parties had grown to 32. This is a considerable number, but it is far fewer than the number of parties to the convention (111 in the summer of 1990) and only half the number of parties (63) that participated in the Second Review Conference. Most industrialized countries and all the permanent members of the Security Council took part, but not a single country in the Middle East, only one country in Africa (Togo), two in Latin America (Chile and Equador), and three in Asia (China, Japan, and North Korea). Many parties probably did not participate in the information exchange because they had nothing to declare or because they gave the exchange very low priority. It is difficult to believe that countries such as India and Brazil have nothing to declare. It should be noted, however, that China, France, and Italy started reporting in 1989, so other parties might start reporting before the Third Review Conference.

Participation in the exchange of information is not the same as full implementation of the agreed-upon measures. Doubts exist whether the parties that took part in the data exchange all noted everything they should have declared. In some cases research establishments involved in protection against chemical and biological weapons were not declared, possibly because the laboratories in question dealt mainly with protection against chemical weapons and thus did not "specialize" in protection against biological weapons.

The scope of three confidence-building measures is defined by the phrase "directly related to the convention." This wording was chosen to paper over the difference between those who wanted the measures to apply only to biological defense research and those who wanted them to apply to infectious disease research in general. As was pointed out above, the meeting of experts did not agree on a common definition of those words. This hampers the measures' effectiveness. This problem will be aggravated if the Third Review Conference decides to extend these measures. It therefore seems useful to examine the phrase more closely.

The convention's text does not offer much help. In Article 5 the phrase "problems which may arise in relation to the objective of . . . the Convention" is used to define the scope of consultation and cooperation. And Article 8 speaks about "extraordinary events, related to the subject matter of the Convention" that might make parties withdraw from the BWC. The phrase "directly related to the Convention" cannot be found in the convention and the final declaration of the First Review Conference. The Second Review Conference picked these deliberately vague words, partly because a precise definition of the measures' scope was not possible in the short duration of the conference, partly to cover up the fact that some Western parties wanted the measures to concentrate on giving information about potentially suspicious activities, while other (socialist and nonaligned) parties believed that broad cooperation in research for civil purposes and so on would by itself build confidence. This difference of opinion on the aim of the measures is nicely illustrated by the introduction to the four measures, which reads as follows (my comments in brackets):

> The Conference, mindful of the provisions of Article V and Article X [mentioning Article 10 argues for a wide scope], and determined to strengthen the authority of the Convention and to enhance confidence in the implementation of its provisions [these two phrases argue for a narrow scope], agrees that the States Parties are to implement, on the basis of mutual co-operation, the following measures, in order to prevent or reduce the occurrence of ambiguities, doubts and suspicions [the narrow aim], and in order to improve international co-operation in the field of peaceful bacteriological (biological) activities [the additional objective of socialist and nonaligned parties].[24]

The meeting of experts was supposed to deal with the details of the measures, but it only partly overcame the differences of opinion. It did agree on a very narrow interpretation of laboratories that "specialize in permitted biological activities directly related to the Convention" but did not clarify the meaning of "directly related to the Convention" in the third and fourth measures. Somebody might argue that the narrow interpretation of the second part of the first measure did not result from a narrow interpretation of "directly related to the Convention" but from a definition of "permitted biological activities" as "activities for prophylactic or protective purposes against possible hostile use of biological agents or toxins."[25] But this definition of "permitted" is neither self-evident nor generally accepted. In the 1983 report of the ad hoc working group on chemical weapons to the Committee on Disarmament, for example, "permitted purposes" is defined as "(i) non-hostile purposes, that is industrial, agricultural, research, medical, law enforcement, or other peaceful purposes, or protective purposes" and "(ii) military purposes which are not related to the use of chemical weapons."[26]

In the draft convention on the prohibition of chemical weapons introduced by then Vice President George Bush in 1984, a comparable definition was given:

> "Permitted purposes" means industrial, agricultural, research, medical or other peaceful purposes; protective purposes; and military purposes that do not make use of the chemical action of a toxic chemical to interfere directly with normal functioning of man and animals so as to cause death, temporary incapacitation or permanent damage.

"Permitted" is not likely to be used in such an unusually restricted manner. Thus the phrase "related to the Convention" is interpreted more narrowly here than in the other measures.

Lack of Feedback

The confidence-building measures agreed upon are, on closer scrutiny, complicated and often vague, leaving ample room for different interpretations. Such differences have hampered comparison of the data and reduced the confidence in the data provided. In some cases doubts have been expressed about whether parties were implementing the measures in good faith. A spokesman of the Soviet Union, for example, stated on February 2, 1989: "As to the United

States, it manifested the strange 'forgetfulness' in 1987 and 1988. It either did not report to the United Nations about its research centers or laboratories . . . or it provided incomplete information, or else it made unjustifiably long delays about providing such information. . . . "[27]

No mechanism is functioning to resolve misunderstandings about the information provided. (A consultative meeting open to all states parties could play such a role, but has never been convened.) This lack also complicates evaluation of the clarity of the information parties provide, as they do not receive any direct feedback on this information.

All information is to be provided "in one of the authentic languages of the Convention" to the UN Department for Disarmament Affairs and forwarded "in the form received" to all states parties.[28] For many parties, however, information received in Chinese or Russian will hardly build any confidence.

Unusual Outbreaks of Diseases

Until 1989 no information had been exchanged on unusual outbreaks of diseases. Nevertheless, unusual outbreaks did, of course, take place. No good reasons exist to believe that any of these outbreaks was connected with biological weapons research, because, ironically, the occurrence of unusual outbreaks of diseases is in itself not unusual. An example was the discovery of the deadly Ebola virus among monkeys imported into the United States from the Philippines in November 1989.[29] The carcasses of the infected monkeys were brought to Fort Detrick (a research institute in Frederick, Maryland, financed by the U.S. Department of Defense) for examination. Later it became known that at least one monkey handler may have been infected with the virus.[30] A citizen of Frederick seized upon this affair to argue for more information "about what was going on in laboratories . . . especially in the Department of Defense labs, including contractors for the DOD that are doing research with hazardous organisms and toxins."[31]

Perhaps no party declared any unusual outbreak through 1989 because parties felt that, in the absence of any other reports, a single report to the UN Department for Disarmament Affairs on such an outbreak would stimulate allegations that the outbreak was linked to accidents with biological weapons rather than build confidence.[32]

Verification

Finally, the confidence-building measures are not suited for solving concrete doubts. Only a verification regime could possibly do that. Under Article 6 of the convention, parties may lodge a complaint with the Security Council and undertake "to co-operate in carrying out any investigation which the Security Council may initiate" on the basis of such a complaint. This provision could be considered as opening the possibility of verification, but it is clearly insufficient, since the permanent members of the Security Council could veto any unwelcome investigation (unless the Security Council agreed to consider the initiation of an investigation as a procedural matter). Moreover, the obligation "to co-operate in carrying out any investigation" is too loosely worded to ensure that in the case of serious allegations an inspection team would indeed be allowed to inspect everything necessary to reveal the truth.

3

The Chemical Weapons Convention as a Model for the Biological Weapons Convention

It is generally expected that a verification regime to strengthen the Biological Weapons Convention should to a large extent be modeled after the verification regime of the Chemical Weapons Convention currently being negotiated in Geneva. But so far little thought has been given to how this could be done, mainly because it is difficult to tell what exactly should be taken as a model as long as no agreement has been reached, not only on the details, but even on some of the basic concepts underlying the CWC.

But now that the chemical weapons negotiations seem to be in their final stage and the Third BWC Review Conference is approaching, it seems both possible and useful to describe in general terms how the verification regime of the CWC, as it has been developed so far, could be used as a model for the BWC. After a short overview of the main features of the CWC, this chapter identifies the concepts underlying the convention and finally considers whether these elements and concepts can be relevant for a possible BWC verification regime.

The CWC's Basic Structure

The projected chemical weapons convention consists of the following five main parts:

1. The central provision prohibits parties to develop, produce, retain, transfer, and use chemical weapons.

2. As a logical consequence of this ban, parties are obliged to declare, seal, and destroy chemical weapon stocks and chemical weapon production plants. This will take place under a regime of international on-site inspection.

3. The chemical industry (or an important part of it) will be subjected to obligatory declarations and routine on-site inspections to verify the accuracy of the declarations and compliance with the convention. (The key precursors of chemical warfare agents are made in the civil chemical industry, and civil chemical plants often have the capability to produce warfare agents.)[1]

4. Parties have the right to request inspection of any suspected location or facility on the territory of another party. These challenge inspections can take place anytime, everywhere, at very short notice, and can never be refused. No consensus has yet been reached on this innovative proposal made by then Vice President Bush.

5. The inspections will be carried out by the international inspectors of the technical secretariat. This technical secretariat will be part of an international organization for the implementation of the convention. The highest organ in this organization will be the conference of (all) states parties, but an executive council (with limited membership) will supervise the implementation of the convention on a more frequent basis.

Routine Inspection of the
Chemical Industry

The most complicated part of the CWC is the routine verification of the civil chemical industry. The envisaged regime could be described as consisting of two parts that have not been developed in parallel, but consecutively. Originally it was planned that the international inspectorate would concentrate its efforts on the chemicals that, from a technical point of view, presented the largest risk. Later this approach was considered insufficient, and a complementary regime was proposed that would cover the whole chemical industry.

A Classification of Chemicals

The first system of verification was built upon a classification of the most relevant chemicals according to their risk (and, as a secondary criterion, according to their civil use) into three "schedules" subjected to three different regimes. All three schedules contain chemicals that can be used as warfare agents and precursors of such agents. Schedule 1 contains the most dangerous compounds that are very suited for weapon purposes and have no permitted applications except in very small (gram) quantities. Schedule 2 contains chemicals that present a somewhat smaller risk and are often produced in small commercial quantities. Schedule 3 contains chemicals that are considered to present an even smaller but still substantial risk and are produced in large quantities (sometimes even more than 100,000 tons).

It should be added here that an intrinsic tension exists between the criteria of risk and civil use. According to the criterion of civil use (or, to be more precise, nonprohibited use), a chemical should be moved to a less intrusive inspection regime if civil production would grow significantly. But the risk that the compound would be used for chemical weapons purposes would grow, rather than diminish, if larger quantities were in circulation. So the risk criterion would argue for maintaining (if not strengthening) the verification regime for the compound.

Production, storage, and use of the chemicals on Schedule 1 is permitted only for a limited number of purposes (such as research and protection against chemical weapons) and even then only in very small quantities under strict rules of declaration and inspection. The most important chemicals classified as Schedule 1 are the nerve agents, the mustard gases, and a few key precursors for binary nerve agents.[2]

Production and use of the chemicals listed on Schedule

2 for other purposes than chemical weapons is not subjected to limitations, but if the quantity is above a certain threshold, the party must declare the facility and allow on-site inspections. On Schedule 2 are mainly key precursors of the agents on Schedule 1. Commercial use of Schedule 2 chemicals is usually small.

Civil production of Schedule 3 chemicals is so large that it was not considered feasible to verify declarations of such production.[3] The regime for these chemicals is therefore limited to an obligation to report to the technical secretariat the quantities and purpose of production and use. Among the chemicals on Schedule 3 are toxic chemicals that have been used as warfare agents, such as hydrogen cyanide and phosgene, and widely used precursors, such as phosphorus oxychloride and sulphur dichloride.

Ad Hoc Inspections

The system described above encompasses only production plants that produce, process, or use chemicals on one of the three lists, even though many other plants have similar capabilities. Because of the large variety of chemical plants and the diversity of chemical warfare agents, no clear and objective criteria can be devised to distinguish plants that are capable of producing chemical weapons from plants that are not.

Western countries have therefore proposed that the whole chemical industry be brought under a regime of routine ad hoc inspections as a supplement to the more intrusive routine inspections of plants that are declared as producing Schedule 2 chemicals. The only purpose of these inspections would be to verify whether, at the time of the inspection, any chemicals on one of the lists was produced without being reported. The plants to be inspected would be chosen on the basis of a register of all chemical plants, either by the international technical secretariat or by the states parties. The number of inspections a party would be allowed to request in a year could be limited by quota, just as the number of ad hoc inspections a party would have to allow.

In the winter of 1990–1991, the Swedish delegation informally proposed a combination of the regimes for Schedules 2 and 3 and the concept of ad hoc inspections. Chemical plants would have to be declared in case chemicals on Schedules 2 or 3 were produced in quantities above certain thresholds and in case one of a number of specially identified chemical conversion processes were used. The latter category would cover plants that do not produce relevant chemicals but have relevant capabilities. All declared plants would be open for short notice on-site inspections to verify the accuracy of declarations and to verify the absence of Schedule 1 chemicals. Each party would have the right to propose 10 declared plants a year for inspection and would be obliged to propose at least one inspection outside its territory. On the basis of these proposals, the technical secretariat would select at random the facilities to be inspected.

Verification of the CWC

The verification regime of the projected Chemical Weapons Convention is based on concepts that are sometimes fundamentally different from the concepts underlying earlier arms control agreements. A clear perception of these concepts seems essential for understanding the CWC and the role it can play as model for strengthening the Biological Weapons Convention.

Single-purpose items (in the case of the CWC) are materials and equipment that were specifically designed for or have no other application than prohibited purposes. Dual-purpose items are materials and equipment that can be used for prohibited purposes but also have applications that are not prohibited. This dichotomy is of fundamental importance for verification. Whereas verifying the destruction of single-purpose items is relatively easy, verification that dual-purpose items are not misused can be very complicated. Possibly the best example of this is the envisaged regime to verify that the chemical industry is not misused to produce chemical weapons. A regime to verify nonproduction of biological weapons in containment laboratories and biotechnological plants might be even more complicated, because much smaller quantities of agent can be militarily relevant, even though the number of such laboratories and plants is probably much smaller than the number of chemical plants. Because the Biological Weapons Convention does not include a verification regime, little effort has been made to distinguish between single and dual-purpose items.

Two Criteria

The principal criterion with which the Chemical Weapons Convention judges the possession and use of dual-purpose items is the purpose for which a party possesses and uses these items. For the Biological Weapons Convention this so-called general-purpose criterion is not just the principal, but the only, criterion. But the general-purpose criterion is a subjective one that is very difficult to verify. In only a few cases, such as actual use, do the facts leave no room for excuses and pretexts. To make verification of the Chemical Weapons Convention feasible, another criterion had to be found. Routine verification of non-misuse of dual-purpose items in the Chemical Weapons Convention is therefore not directly based on the (subjective) purpose of the possessor or user but on facts. In other words, an inspection team does not verify whether the intentions of a party are legitimate or not; it determines whether a party has correctly declared what it had to declare and did not hide anything that should be declared or is prohibited. Such a regime would be possible for the BWC.

Ideally a regime for routine verification would guarantee the timely detection of violations. But what is a violation? The concealment of one chemical warfare shell by a souvenir collector would, for example, technically violate the convention. But even the most intrusive verification regime would never give 100 percent certainty that such a violation would be quickly detected. One could use this example as a pretext to question the verifiability of the Chemical Weapons Convention, but a more sensible question would be, "So what?" Such a violation would threaten only the family of the souvenir collector and their neighbors, and it would be unwise to judge the verifiability of the convention on that basis.

Here the concept of militarily relevant quantities should be added. The purpose of verification would then be more aptly described as guaranteeing the timely detection of militarily relevant violations. This would exclude small technical irregularities, but it begs the question of how a militarily relevant quantity should be defined. Definitions of a militarily relevant quantity of chemical warfare agents range from 80 to 1,000 tons, depending, among other things, on the lethality of the agents. As some toxins are much more toxic than the usual chemical warfare agents, a militarily relevant quantity might be smaller than that. A militarily relevant quantity of biological agents would be even smaller than that (because they reproduce themselves in the body of the victim), but how small is difficult to say. The history of biological weapons does, however, give some indications. In 1944 British experts estimated that a hypothetical retaliatory attack on six German cities would require 1,300 tons of a slurry containing 4 percent anthrax spores.[4] That was based on the assumption that 930 kilograms per square kilometer would be needed to cause 50 percent lethality. Over time the efficiency of spreading the agent grew. In 1960 U.S. experts concluded that 7.1 kilograms per square kilometer would be sufficient to cause more than 60 percent casualties. For Q-fever even 0.08 kg/km^2 would be sufficient.[5]

Verification is usually considered in absolute terms. The higher the degree of certainty an inspection regime provides, the better it is thought to be. Very little attention is given to cost considerations. Now the ritual significance of, for example, intrusive inspection of sealing and destroying declared stocks (of chemical weapons, for example, or cruise missiles) should not be underestimated, but the marginal utility of intensive verification of such facilities depends on the chance that stockpiles at undeclared facilities will remain undetected. The cost effectiveness of routinely inspecting declared facilities would be best if the risk of being caught red-handed by such inspections were considered so large that parties refrained from using declared facilities for prohibited activities. Making routine verification more effective than that is fine, but superfluous, unless at the same time the inspection regime for undeclared facilities were strengthened.

The purpose of most verification regimes is the timely detection of militarily relevant violations. This description pertains to verifying the nonremoval and destruction of chemical weapons stockpiles. The material accountancy system used by the International Atomic Energy Agency (IAEA) to verify that nuclear plants are not used for nuclear weapons purposes is another example of such a regime.[6] The regime for routine verification of nonproduction of chemical weapons in the chemical industry was originally modeled after the IAEA's material accountancy system. It gradually became clear, however, that a material accountancy system for all relevant chemicals was infeasible, and a material accountancy system for the most relevant chemicals would at best give confidence about some facilities, but no guarantee at all about others. The number of plants that could, with more or less difficulty, be used for producing chemical warfare agents is so large, and the civil production of relevant chemicals is so enormous, that a routine verification regime that would guarantee the timely detection of any significant violation would be excessively expensive.

Acknowledgment that such a regime would be impractical led to a reappraisal of the purpose of verification. According to the new concept, verification is to give confidence in compliance by deterring violations. To deter a country from violating the convention, the chance of being caught through routine inspections does not have to be 100 percent. The purpose of routine inspection of the chemical industry – to deter violations at declared facilities by chance of detection – can also be stated more positively as building confidence in compliance by declaring chemical plants and opening them for inspection.

Unless undeclared facilities can be easily detected by a system of material accountancy or by national technical means, a regime for inspecting undeclared facilities is an indispensable complement to a routine verification regime. An effective system of material accountancy for the Biological Weapons Convention is out of the question, and very few countries have national technical means to speak of, so if the Biological Weapons Convention is strengthened with a verification protocol, a regime for challenge inspection of undeclared facilities will have to be part of it.

Inspection of declared facilities has advantages over inspection of undeclared facilities for both the inspectorate and the inspected party. Both know more or less what to expect. The details of how an inspection is conducted can even be recorded in a facility attachment. Inspection of an undeclared facility conversely might entail unexpected problems for both sides, but mostly for the inspected party. The inspected facility might contain very sensitive technology, or highly classified information, that has no relation to the objective of the inspection but that could not easily be concealed from an inspection team. In the specific case of the United States, the Fourth Amendment to the Constitution presents an additional problem, as it limits the possibility of inspections of private property. For this reason on-site inspection of undeclared facilities is not popular, and arms control agreements usually do not contain a regime for on-site inspection of undeclared facilities, or if they contain such a regime, parties have refrained from invoking it.[7]

The important exception is the regime for inspections provided for in the Document of the Stockholm Conference on confidence- and security-building measures.[8] This agreement deals with areas rather than with facilities, however, and parties are allowed to deny access to "areas or sensitive points to which access is normally denied or restricted, military and other defence installations, as well as naval vessels, military vehicles and aircraft."[9] Such exclusions do not make this verification regime useless because the dimensions of the items that an inspection team would look for are as large as military activities involving at least 3,000 troops or 300 battle tanks.[10]

In the case of the Chemical Weapons Convention, the circumstances are quite different. Military maneuvers involving 300 tanks cannot possibly be held within a very large building. But production of militarily relevant quantities of chemical weapons could very well take place there. A regime for inspecting undeclared facilities to verify compliance with the Chemical Weapons Convention could not afford, therefore, to exclude any buildings or installations just because they were of a sensitive or military nature. If such exceptions were allowed, all chemical weapons plants and stockpiles could easily be excluded from inspection. The regime for challenge inspections foreseen (but not yet fully agreed) for the Chemical Weapons Convention is by necessity the most radical and intrusive verification regime that has ever been proposed. (There are, however, rumors that the United States has second thoughts about challenge inspections in this radical form, although the concept was proposed by George Bush himself.)[11]

An Example for the BWC

The following paragraphs discuss the relevance of several elements of the CWC's verification regime to a possible verification regime for the BWC.

All parties to the BWC undertook to destroy, or divert to peaceful purposes, all their biological weapons within nine months after the convention went into effect, so a regime for verifying destruction of biological weapons would be relevant only if a country with such weapons becomes party to the convention.[12]

In contrast with the envisaged CWC, the BWC does not oblige parties to destroy the production equipment for the weapons. A verification regime is therefore not needed.[13]

Both the BWC and the projected CWC permit production of even the most dangerous agents for a number of purposes. But the CWC sets much stricter limits to such production than does the BWC. This becomes clear when the single regime of the BWC is compared with the special regime of the CWC for the most dangerous agents (see table 2). It would seem that this envisaged regime of the CWC might serve as a model for a regime to verify that the most dangerous biological agents and toxins are produced only for nonprohibited purposes.

Most elements of the regime can, in an adapted form, probably be taken over:

- A list of the most risky biological agents and toxins.
- Guidelines and procedures for changing the list. The current "Annex on Chemicals" in the rolling text of the CWC contains guidelines for revision of the schedules.[14]
- A more precisely defined limitation of the purposes for which the agents on the list may be produced, conserved, and used. The term "peaceful" should be avoided and be replaced by such wording as "research, medical, and pharmaceutical."
- A binding obligation to declare every facility where any of the agents on the lists is produced, stored, or used, irrespective of the quantity involved (but not including facilities where these agents are present accidentally, such as hospitals).
- Routine on-site inspection of these facilities to verify the accuracy of declarations.

TABLE 2
Comparison of BWC and CWC Limits
on Most Dangerous Agents

	Biological Weapons Convention	Chemical Weapons Convention
Scope	All biological agents and toxins	Chemicals listed in Schedule 1
Qualitative Limitations	"For prophylactic, protective or other peaceful purposes"	"Research, medical, pharmaceutical, or protective purposes"[15]
Quantitative Limitations	Types and quantities justified for such purposes, without a maximum	Types and quantities justified for such purposes, but the aggregate amount should be equal to or less than 1 metric ton
Number of Facilities	No limitations	a. One single small-scale facility (SSSF) b. One production facility for protective purposes (production limited to 10 kilograms) c. Production facilities (approved by government) for research, medical, or pharmaceutical purposes (maximum 10 kilograms per facility)[16] d. Laboratories for research, medical, or pharmaceutical purposes (maximum 100 grams per year)
Routine Verification	No	a, b, and c shall be subject to international on-site inspection and monitoring with on-site instruments;[17] d shall not be subjected to routine inspections
Challenge Inspections	No	Yes

• A concrete limit on the amount that may be produced. Such a limit should be a fraction of the limits for chemical warfare agents – for example, 10 grams instead of 1 ton and milligrams instead of grams.

• Strict rules for the production, storage, and use of the agents on the list (for example, good laboratory practice, standardization of containment levels) and minimum requirements for protection levels.

• International inspection to verify compliance with these rules.

It would be naive to think that transposing the regime for Schedule 1 chemicals to a list of biological agents and toxins would be simple. Certainly many problems will surface. These problems might be identified by simulating implementation of the regime. Such trial inspections have proven to be indispensable to negotiations on other arms control agreements, such as the Chemical Weapons Convention. During trial inspections at chemical plants, several of the concepts developed in the negotiations proved completely unrealistic.

An example is the definition of the object of inspection: the facility or, more precisely, a production unit. It was argued, and not contradicted in Geneva, that all the pipelines leading to and from the production vessel would be considered part of the production unit to be inspected. But during trial inspection visits to plants in the Netherlands, it became clear that several production units are directly connected by pipes with other production units at other industrial complexes, sometimes dozens of kilometers away. Another thing learned during visits to the plants was that some biotechnological plants were building multipurpose containment facilities that they intended to use primarily to protect research, development, and production of new products from outside influences but that also could be used to contain work with agents that can be dangerous for the outside world. As long as biotechnological plants use these containment facilities only to protect their products, they do not need special permission from the government. Such facilities nevertheless present a potential capability for work relevant to the BWC.

One could ask whether it is feasible to verify the accuracy of declarations about production and use of agents on the list. The answer is probably no. If a party declares it has 10 grams of a listed agent, but in reality it has concealed 200 grams, possibly under a false name, an inspection team would have a hard time finding it without turning the whole facility upside down.

But does this mean forgetting about using the example of Schedule 1 of the CWC as a model for verifying the Biological Weapons Convention? Again the answer is no. Just as in the case of the CWC, the criterion for judging the feasibility of inspection is not whether small anomalies will be found with certainty (verifying whether a facility retains 10 or 200 grams of the nerve agent VX is also very difficult), but whether listed agents are present and whether declared agents are present in quantities far larger than declared. Of course, the characteristic features of biological agents have to be taken into consideration. Verification of the BWC will be more difficult than verification of the CWC because militarily relevant quantities are much smaller. The allowed quantities should be very small, even if compliance would be difficult to verify, if no legitimate purpose exists for larger quantities.

Production of vaccines against listed agents may require relatively large quantities, but a strict verification regime should apply. This regime could be modeled after the verification regime for Schedule 2 chemicals. The Chemical Weapons Convention will not limit production or use of these compounds for nonprohibited purposes, but production and use will have to be declared and these declarations verified.

In addition, it could be considered to distribute biological agents and toxins according to their risk over a number of lists with different regimes, following the example of the three schedules of the Chemical Weapons Convention. The

essence of the regimes for the chemicals on the three schedules is as follows:

	Declaration	Routine Verification	Production Limits
Schedule 1	Yes	Yes	1 metric ton
Schedule 2	Yes	Yes	No
Schedule 3	Yes	No	No

The production limit of 1 metric ton should of course be
much smaller in the case of biological agents.

As explained above, it is infeasible to verify the Chemical Weapons Convention by a system of material accountancy for all relevant compounds. This infeasibility holds
even more for the Biological Weapons Convention. A regime
to verify that production equipment is not misused for biological weapons purposes will therefore have to be the cen-
terpiece of any routine verification regime for the Biological
Weapons Convention. In developing such a regime the CWC
can be both a negative and a positive example.

The Chemical Weapons Convention is a negative example for the Biological Weapons Convention because it has
taken the negotiators about 15 years to realize that a verification regime limited to declaration and inspection of the
production and use of the most dangerous key precursors
will not deal with many of the most risky facilities. As this
regime has been adopted in the rolling text, it is very difficult to change it. It is nevertheless hoped that it will prove
possible to replace it with a regime that covers all relevant
facilities. But now that the builders of a verification regime
for the Biological Weapons Convention have the choice,
they should choose the preferred approach straight away.

In retrospect a two-edged approach might have been
advisable; an approach in which not only the most risky
chemicals, but also the most risky production equipment,
would have been listed in schedules. Such an approach
would have had two advantages. First, a routine verifica-

tion regime based on declaration of both the most dangerous chemicals and the most risky equipment would have more adequately encompassed the plants that present the largest risk than a regime based solely on declaration of chemicals.

Second, the accuracy of declarations of equipment is much easier to verify than the accuracy of declarations of chemicals. Take an imaginary example of a chemical plant that secretly was producing chemical warfare agents, and assume that the plant was registered as a chemical plant, so that the ad hoc inspection regime would apply. If an ad hoc inspection were announced, the inspected party would quickly try to remove or destroy all undeclared stocks of relevant chemicals. It is very doubtful that this could be accomplished without leaving any traces. If good preparations were made, however, such as using equipment that is specially designed for quick cleaning, it is conceivable that the inspection team would find the plant in a suspicious condition but without clear evidence of a violation. It is unthinkable, however, that the special production equipment could be concealed in the few hours between announcement of the inspection and arrival of the inspection team. If a routine verification regime had existed for such special production equipment, the country would have had to choose between declaring the equipment (resulting in relatively frequent routine inspections) and not declaring it (with a good chance that it would be caught during an ad hoc inspection or a challenge inspection). Confronted with these two unattractive options, the country might be dissuaded from making chemical weapons or at least feel forced to forgo both options and produce the agents outside its existing chemical industry, which would be more costly and time consuming and more easily recognized with national technical means.

The Chemical Weapons Convention also can serve as a model, because the envisaged verification regime might, in an adapted form, be very suitable for the BWC. As relevant quantities of biological warfare agents are small and can probably be destroyed quickly, it would seem that a verification regime based on an obligation to declare both relevant equipment and relevant agents might hold out the best prospects of success.

Prohibition of Development and Inspection
of Laboratories

It is remarkable that in the negotiations on a Chemical Weapons Convention – considered by many as the model for verification – so far no serious attempt has been made to formulate measures to build confidence that parties comply with the ban on development of chemical weapons. As a result, the ban on development risks becoming a dead letter. In the case of the Chemical Weapons Convention, that might not be fatal for the convention as a whole, as production of militarily relevant quantities is not possible in a research and development facility (except for some toxins and similar materials). Production of a relevant quantity of biological weapons, however, might take place in a laboratory.

We are confronted here with two problems. The first is that both the Chemical Weapons Convention and the Biological Weapons Convention prohibit development but do not provide for any routine measure to verify compliance with this prohibition. The second problem is that a militarily relevant quantity of biological warfare agents can be so small that it probably can be produced in a research establishment. This problem was never tackled seriously because verification of nonproduction was considered to give sufficient certainty that a party would not be able to acquire a militarily relevant stockpile of chemical weapons and, most of all, because verification of nondevelopment would have involved inspection of very sensitive chemical research and development facilities. Furthermore, a clear definition of development would have been required to distinguish it from research. As was set out above, making this distinction would have been difficult, but a solution would not have been beyond human ingenuity.[18]

The second problem, the fact that militarily relevant quantities of biological warfare agents can probably be produced at research establishments, implies that the Biological Weapons Convention cannot afford to ignore the problem of inspection of research establishments. It is not easy to decide, however, how much of a biological agent would constitute a militarily relevant quantity. As the victims of a biological weapon attack will not properly line up to become infected, large amounts of agents might be needed, especially if consistent and widespread results are required.

It should be added that the projected Chemical Weapons Convention does constrain chemicals known to present the largest risk. These chemicals, listed on Schedule 1, may be produced for research purposes, but every laboratory that produces or uses more than 100 grams should be declared. And the total volume of all chemicals on this list in a country in a given year may never exceed 1 metric ton. This regime does not, however, verify nondevelopment of chemical warfare agents, because Schedule 1 necessarily contains little more than the well-known chemical warfare agents, not the agents still in development. The best way to provide confidence that no clandestine research and development of biological weapons is taking place is complete openness of all relevant research. I recognize that many interests, commercial, military and others, argue against such openness, but the supreme interest of preventing biological warfare should prevail.

Challenge Inspections

A verification regime for undeclared facilities will of necessity have a nonroutine character and should encompass all locations and facilities that could be considered relevant. The regime for challenge inspections envisaged for the Chemical Weapons Convention could be a model for the

Biological Weapons Convention, as the main problems are the same. A country that is secretly violating the convention will do whatever it can to prevent a challenge inspection at the location of the violation. It is therefore essential that parties have no legal possibility for refusing a challenge inspection and that a refusal is considered as proof of violation.

But the first question that has to be answered is, what would a challenge inspection try to verify? And again the problem is that the Biological Weapons Convention was not designed with verification in mind. The convention does not prohibit any activity unequivocally but in essence prohibits certain activities only if they "have no justification" for permitted purposes. This makes life very hard for an inspection team, because it is not enough to prove that potential biological warfare agents were developed, produced, stockpiled, acquired, or retained. The inspection team also will have to refute the claim of the inspected country that the activities were justified for permitted purposes. Even when such a claim has very little credibility, it might be very difficult to find conclusive evidence that the claim is false.

The core of the problem is that the Biological Weapons Convention does not prohibit concrete activities but only activities with unjustified intentions. In some cases (for example, a bunker full of biological weapons), there is no room for doubts, but if a challenge inspection regime or any other verification regime is to make real sense, this situation should be changed. The subjective obligations and prohibitions of the convention will have to be complemented with objective and operational requirements.

An International Verification Organization

As long as the international data exchange remains as it is now and verification is limited to occasional ad hoc teams sent out by the secretary general to verify allegations of use of chemical and toxin weapons, the existing machinery of the United Nations might be sufficient. Nevertheless, even now the UN Department for Disarmament Affairs cannot deal with the data exchange in the most effective way. Even without widening the scope of the data exchange, it would seem advisable to let the UN Department for Disarmament Affairs play a more active role in the data exchange.

If parties would agree to open their declared facilities for very infrequent international inspections, a list of international experts to draw upon for ad hoc inspection teams might be sufficient. But if such inspections became more routine, this list of inspectors might slowly evolve into an embryonic international inspectorate. As explained elsewhere in this book, an effective implementation of confidence-building measures would be helped by yearly consultations among parties about the practical problems involved. The consultative meetings of experts, envisaged by the review conferences, might serve this purpose. The Third Review Conference could request its bureau to convene such meetings regularly.

The institutionalization of a machinery to implement the agreed-upon measures could proceed on a step-by-step basis. At some point, the question will have to be addressed whether a special international organization should be set up for this purpose or whether an existing organization should be used. A possible candidate would be the international organization that will be set up to implement the Chemical Weapons Convention. The precedent for such a setup is the role of the IAEA in conducting inspections in the framework of the nuclear Non-Proliferation Treaty. The IAEA has its own statute and in fact even predates the Non-Proliferation Treaty. But it would probably be unacceptable if the parties to the Chemical Weapons Convention could decide on the implementation of the Biological Weapons Convention without being party to it, while countries party only to the Biological Weapons Convention could not decide on its implementation. The solution might be to establish a separate executive board within the organization to oversee the verification of the Biological Weapons Convention.

Protecting Confidential Information

If the scope of the data exchange were expanded and supplemented with a regime to verify the accuracy of the declarations, rules would have to be developed to assure the inspected countries, institutes, and companies that their military, commercial, and technical secrets would not be compromised. To give such assurance, a special Annex on the Protection of Confidential Information was added to the draft text of the Chemical Weapons Convention.[19] This annex consists of four parts:

- General principles for the handling of confidential information, such as criteria for classification and publication
- Employment and conduct of personnel in the technical secretariat, such as limiting access to confidential information
- Measures to protect sensitive installations and prevent disclosure of confidential data. The inspected party may also propose such measures, but the inspection team has to adopt such proposals only when it considers them appropriate
- Procedures in case of breaches or alleged breaches of confidentiality. In serious cases the diplomatic immunity of inspectors may be waived by the director general of the technical secretariat.

Protection of confidential information is also ensured by the following provisions in the envisaged Chemical Weapons Convention:

- A state will be inspected only by inspectors who were previously accepted, silently or explicitly, by that state.
- All inspections will be conducted according to the rules of an elaborate inspection protocol.
- Routine inspections (with the possible exception of the less intrusive ad hoc inspections) will be based on a specific agreement (a so-called facility attachment) that will be negotiated between the technical secretariat and the in-

spected party on the basis of a model agreement that is appended to the convention.

If a verification regime were to be added to the Biological Weapons Convention, these rules and regulations could probably be taken largely from the CWC.

The Need for Flexibility

A verification regime modeled after that of the Chemical Weapons Convention will by necessity include many small details, such as precise definitions of the items that are to be verified and elaborate verification procedures. As scientific and technological developments proceed, some of these details will need revision. Strict amendment procedures that require the explicit consent of all parties might be needed for the basic provisions of the convention, but they should not prevent adjustment of the detailed verification provisions.

The Chemical Weapons Convention will therefore set different rules for revising different parts of the convention and its annexes. What the amendment and revision procedures will look like is not yet precisely known, but probably the three following types of procedures will be instituted:[20]

- When adopted by an amendment conference with no party casting a negative vote and ratified by all parties casting a positive vote, the amendment will enter into force for all parties. This difficult amendment procedure would apply for the fundamental obligations of the convention, such as the obligation to destroy all stocks within 10 years.
- According to the simplified amendment procedure, a proposal would be considered approved if no more than x parties objected to a recommendation by the executive council. If this were the case, the conference of states parties would take a decision by qualified majority.
- For additions to and deletions from the lists of items

that are subjected to verification, an even simpler procedure would apply. A proposal of any party would be adopted if no party objected within a certain time. In case a party objected, the second procedure mentioned would apply.

A verification regime for the Biological Weapons Convention should provide for lighter rules for amending the details of that regime than the rules in Article 11 of the convention. These rules could probably be modeled after the above-mentioned simplified amendment procedures.

Many lessons can be drawn from the negotiations on a Chemical Weapons Convention that can be useful for a verification protocol to the Biological Weapons Convention. It should always be remembered, however, that biological agents differ fundamentally from chemical agents and that the objects of verification – such as potential production facilities – differ also. The most fruitful way to test how useful the experience of the CWC negotiations would be for the BWC is to use the concepts in trial inspections of BWC-relevant facilities.

4

What Can Be Done?

The earlier chapters suggested possible measures to strengthen the convention. This chapter summarizes these measures and adds a few others. First, it examines whether the existing provisions are as effective as they could be and then considers whether additional measures could strengthen the existing confidence-building measures. Finally, it discusses the possibilities of a verification regime for the convention. Note that the list of suggestions made in this and previous parts of this book is far from comprehensive. For additional material, I draw the attention of the reader to the proposals of the Working Group on Biological and Toxin Weapons Verification of the Federation of American Scientists.[1] One does not have to agree with every suggestion to agree that these reports are an important contribution to the discussion about strengthening the BWC.

Use Existing Provisions

Even a perfect ban cannot be completely adequate if some relevant states do not subscribe to it. Although more than 110 states are party to the BWC, many states are not. Some countries did not become party because their small bureaucratic apparatus did not find the time to consider the possibility. The Paris Conference on chemical weapons induced a number of countries to become party to the Geneva Protocol. A comparable action to induce countries to become party to the BWC could be useful. The 12 countries of the European Community during 1990 approached all countries that are not yet party to plead for accession. Similar action by other nations would probably be useful.

Several countries deliberately did not become party. Some of them, like Egypt, Iraq, and Syria, signed the convention but did not ratify it. Others, like Israel, did not even sign it. It is questionable whether any of these countries will become party unless all the other mentioned countries become party. In such cases a regional approach might be necessary, with a view to collective accession to the convention. This will be far from easy because of the very difficult relations between these countries.

For countries with serious doubts about the efficacy of the convention, strengthening the convention would make it more attractive. It also could be considered to provide more visible meaning to the commitment under Article 10 to promote cooperation for peaceful purposes, although this might strengthen the mistaken view that such promotion is one of the purposes of the convention.[2] And staying outside the convention could be made less attractive by installing severe controls for export of relevant technology to nonparties. It is unlikely, however, that a country would forgo the option of acquiring biological weapons solely because of such inducements.

Why would a country want to keep the option of biological warfare open? One could think of one or more of the following reasons:

- for use as a tactical or strategic weapon (against military targets)
- for terrorism against civilians, inside or outside the country
- for use as a deterrent against biological weapons

The fact that most countries did become party to the BWC testifies to the weakness of these arguments; the reason several countries in the Middle East signed the convention but not did not ratify it is probably not because they planned to acquire a capability but merely because Israel did not want to become party. Israel did not want to become party because it doubted that other countries in the region would honor their obligations. Any effort to make the countries of the Middle East join the convention will therefore have to start with Israel. The case can easily be argued that even a declaratory ban of biological weapons in the Middle East would be in the interest of Israel. What would be the sense of threatening to use biological weapons against a dictator who is not interested in the lives of his own countrymen? But accession to the convention of all missing countries would not suffice. The convention should also be complied with. That is why a verification protocol might be essential to an effective ban of biological weapons.

Encourage Participation

About two-thirds of all parties did not participate in the data exchange during the first four years after the data exchange was agreed upon. The number of parties that have not implemented the agreement to send the UN Department for Disarmament Affairs information on their national laws or regulations is even larger. As the confidence derived from the confidence-building measures depends completely on the measures being implemented, parties that have not taken part in the information exchange should be encouraged to do so.

It is quite natural that the way the measures were implemented has left much room for improvement, as the data exchange was a new procedure that had to be learned.[3] A forum should be created to discuss implementation, to clarify obscurities, and to improve the information exchange. The consultative meetings foreseen by the review conferences could play this role.

Improve Data Processing

The information provided by parties to the UN Department for Disarmament Affairs (DDA) is forwarded to parties in the form received. The accessibility of the information could be easily improved if the department played a more active role in processing the data. For example, the department could provide, on request, translations of all information received. This would produce extra work for the DDA. It should be discussed whether this cost could be absorbed by redefining the priorities of the department or if it would require extra money.

Reinforce Current Confidence-Building Measures

According to a widespread misunderstanding, arms control does not cost any money. That might be true for an agreement that bans nonexisting weapons and accordingly does not require any measures to assure parties of compliance, but if an agreement deals with weapons that are considered a real threat (as is increasingly the case with biological weapons), then a mechanism has to be developed that helps to build confidence in compliance. Even the smallest possible mechanism costs money. The Second Review Conference ignored this. The role assigned to the DDA is therefore very limited (no translation, no processing) because the services rendered by the UN to enable parties to implement relevant parts of the final declaration of the review conference were supposed to "have no financial implications for the regular budget of the United Nations."[4] It is difficult to require the DDA to play a more active role unless its priorities are redefined or money is made available specifically for that purpose. If a more effective functioning of the current measures is desired, and even more so when the next review conference decides on supplementary measures, states parties will have to pay for it. They could do that, for example, by instituting a special fund for implementing the BWC, by agreeing on a larger budget for the UN Department of Disarmament Affairs, or simply by bringing the costs under the costs of the review conferences.

A mechanism should be devised to provide parties with some feedback on the information they have given and to discuss eventual problems in implementing the measures. In theory such discussion could take place at the review conferences, but the interval between review conferences is too long.

Possibly the best solution would be to convene an annual consultative meeting open to all parties. On the basis of Article 5 of the convention, the First and Second Review Conferences have worked out the possibility of convening such a consultative meeting. Until now such a meeting has never been requested. Although they were originally meant to have an ad hoc character and be used mainly in cases of doubts about compliance, other good use could be made of the meetings now that the confidence-building measures have given a more routine character to implementing the convention. The working methods and rules of procedure of these consultative meetings might draw useful lessons from the Conflict Prevention Center that has been created by the states that participate in the Conference on Security and Cooperation in Europe (CSCE). This Conflict Prevention Center will support and discuss the confidence- and security-building measures (CSBMs) that have been agreed upon by the CSCE participants.

The easiest way to build upon the existing confidence-building measures is to add to their scope.

The Second Review Conference decided that two types of research centers are of special concern: centers with very high containment facilities and centers that specialize in protection against biological weapons. Both categories were defined by the meeting of experts in 1987 in a restrictive way. The main argument for limiting the scope of the data exchange was to avoid biting off more than could be chewed. If the data exchange worked, the scope could be extended at the Third Review Conference.

The meeting of experts decided that laboratories involved in research or development for prophylactic or protective purposes have to be declared only if they have containment units or if they specialize in such work. Confidence in the convention would be strengthened if all laboratories involved in such work were declared, irrespective of whether they have containment units or specialize in this type of work. To disregard whether laboratories had containment units would bring the measure in line with the original agreement at the Second Review Conference.

A laboratory does not have to possess maximum containment facilities to be capable of producing biological warfare agents. Extending the data exchange to a wider range of relevant facilities therefore requires serious consideration. One of the arguments for such an extension is the fact that modern biotechnological plants often possess multipurpose facilities to protect their products from being contaminated by agents in the outside air. These facilities can very easily be used as a maximum containment facility by changing the air-handling system from overpressure (used to keep diseases out) to underpressure (used to keep diseases in). These facilities would satisfy all requirements for a maximum containment facility, but they are not declared, not even to the national government, as long as no dangerous agents are handled.

The best approach to extending the scope of the existing confidence-building measures is to consider anew which types of facilities might give rise to suspicions. I suggest that, apart from the laboratories that are directly involved in protection against biological and toxin weapons, laboratories can be of concern for one or more of the following reasons:

- the types of agents that are handled
- the presence of equipment for producing and conserving microorganisms (such as large-scale fermenters), advanced equipment for harvesting (such as continuous flow centrifuges and filtration techniques), and equipment

for long-term conservation of agents (such as freeze-drying equipment)
  • the facilities for containment.[5]

It seems difficult to strike a happy medium between the current practice of no information and an avalanche of information about every unusual outbreak of disease. One possibility might be to strengthen (if necessary) the reporting system of WHO and to ask WHO to keep the UN Department for Disarmament Affairs informed about unusual outbreaks of diseases. The department would, probably in cooperation with WHO, prepare a yearly summary of unusual outbreaks of diseases for states parties. The working group of the Federation of American Scientists (FAS) suggested that parties should declare all outbreaks of diseases "caused, or possibly caused, by agents" on a list of biological weapons–relevant agents.[6] The attractiveness of this proposal is that it circumvents the problem of defining "unusual." In addition, parties could agree to welcome offers by other parties to participate in analyzing and fighting unusual outbreaks of diseases. Such participation would build confidence that such outbreaks were not caused by biological weapons–related activities.

Implementing the existing data exchange about research establishments is relatively easy because the number of involved establishments is small and the great majority is government-owned.[7] If the scope of the data exchange were widened, the number of facilities involved might grow considerably and might come to encompass many more private facilities. The growth in numbers would require more effective procedures to process the data and make a forum to discuss their implementation indispensable. If such measures were taken, a growth of the number of declared facilities by a factor of 10 would not present insurmountable problems. Whether inclusion of private institutes and companies in the data exchange would present any problems regarding confidential data requires further study. It seems likely that in many countries most of the requested data are already public because of labor safety and environmental protection regulations.

Widen the Scope of the Convention

The list in chapter 2 illustrates that not all activities leading to use of biological weapons are covered by the convention. The activities not covered include research of new warfare agents, building of biological weapon plants, and introduction of biological warfare in military doctrine. Widening the scope of the convention might not seem the highest priority, however, compared with the urgent need to strengthen confidence in compliance with convention as it stands. A clear and comprehensive scope would nevertheless be desirable.

Research directed at the development and production of biological weapons was not included in the scope of the convention because it was considered infeasible to distinguish such research from research directed at permitted purposes. A prohibition of such research would therefore lead to accusations that could be neither validated nor disproved.

In practice, however, a silent consensus seems to exist among parties that offensive research would be a violation of the spirit of the convention. The lack of a formal prohibition has not, for example, prevented the United States from accusing the Soviet Union of violating the convention with research of "the utility of biological weapons."[8] No party has acknowledged that it undertook such research since the convention came into force (neither has a nonparty). The main argument against a prohibition of offensive research is that it is not verifiable. But the real question to be answered is not whether such a prohibition is verifiable but whether the convention would be stronger with or without it. As has been argued above, the stages of research, development, and production of biological warfare agents are difficult to distinguish. It would therefore be useful to leave no doubt that any activity, including research, directed at eventual production and use of biological weapons falls within the scope of the convention. For the same reason the scope should be extended with a clear provision that preparations for use, such as making operational plans for the use of biological weapons, would violate not only the spirit, but also the letter, of the convention. The same holds for preparations for production, such as building a production plant for biological weapons.

Protection and prophylaxis against biological weapons should not be prohibited, but certain constraints and confidence-building measures should be considered – for example, a prohibition to create agents with altered properties that might increase their usefulness as weapons, even for protective purposes.[9]

Finally, it would be useful to include use of biological weapons in the convention's scope and to eliminate any doubts as to whether the convention covers hostile use of animal and plant diseases.

Develop a Verification Regime

The paradox of the exchange of data as a confidence-building measure is that providing information builds confidence but gives rise to questions and, in the longer run, to doubts unless a regime exists to verify the accuracy of the data. It is like the yearly ritual of the affluent in developed countries, when they declare their earnings for the income tax. At the start everybody may give an accurate picture of his or her earnings. But if the accuracy is never verified, it inevitably drops. The attraction of breaking out of the Biological Weapons Convention might seem smaller than the attractiveness of paying less income tax, but the rationale of the convention and the reason for agreeing on confidence-building measures is that this aspect cannot be taken for granted. The convention and the data exchange have decreased the likelihood of biological weapons production, but not excluded it. A verification regime to complement the convention and the data exchange is needed.

The convention is almost unverifiable in its present form because all its obligations depend on the intentions of a party. In almost all controversial cases, a party could argue that its actions were justified by their nonprohibited purpose. A large stockpile of a potential biological warfare agent might, for example, be explained away as a stockpile for several years of vaccine production and large-scale testing of protective measures. The credibility of such arguments might be extremely low; nevertheless, it would be difficult to prove that this explanation was false. Only when biological weapons were used, or were found in the operational stockpiles of standing armed forces, would a party not be able to find a justification.

An effective verification regime requires clear and objective criteria to judge the observed facts. Such criteria could be found by subjecting relevant items to obligatory declaration and quantitative constraints. This does not require amendment of the general purpose criterion of Article 1 of the BWC. As a clear description of the obligations of parties, the criterion is perfect, but it requires an addition to build confidence in compliance.

To illustrate how the basic provisions of such a verification protocol might look, appendix F outlines the main elements of such a protocol. The leading idea behind these elements is simple: (1) the agents and the equipment that are considered to present the largest risk are defined; (2) parties accept certain restrictions on the production and use of these agents and equipment; (3) parties undertake to declare these items, and (4) they accept inspections to verify the accuracy of the provided data. The idea is simple, but to elaborate it into a feasible regime will be difficult. A possible approach is described in the report on the implementation of the FAS proposals.

The purpose of the sketched routine verification regime is not to give complete certainty that every violation will immediately be detected but to give parties confidence that the chance of detection is so large that parties will not dare to produce or stockpile biological weapons at the facilities best equipped for it. Routine verification cannot prevent a party from violating the convention, but it can force the party to take the costly and time-consuming road of building its production facilities in secret, rather than using existing establishments. The hope is that this extra hurdle will make such parties decide not to violate. But if they do, they can still be caught through a challenge inspection.

For clarity, it should be added that this verification regime does not directly verify compliance with Article 1 of the BWC (to avoid a discussion about the justification of activities). In the projected chemical weapons convention, a comparable indirect verification approach is foreseen to verify nonproduction of chemical weapons.

As pointed out earlier, the concept of routine inspection of declared facilities should be well distinguished from the concept of challenge inspections. Such routine inspections are not very different in character from confidence-building visits. But challenge inspections, especially in case of nondeclared facilities, will have a more confrontational character.

The feasibility of a verification regime as has been described here can be ascertained only after a regime has been worked out and tested in trial inspections and when more is known about the number and type of facilities that will have to be inspected. The decisive factors are the technical problems of verification and the costs.

In comparison with the verification of the accuracy of data on listed agents and toxins, the verification of the accuracy of data on relevant equipment and containment measures looks easy. It is unlikely that equipment and containment measures can be destroyed quickly without leaving clear traces. But it remains to be seen whether relevant equipment could be removed efficiently from the site before arrival of an inspection team. Movement of such equipment might be detected, and absence of it might look suspicious. Even when removal of declarable items makes it impossible for an inspection team to find conclusive evidence of a violation, the inspected party would at least have been forced to interrupt its illegal activities. It seems unlikely that these activities could be resumed quickly after the hasty removal of all relevant equipment from the site, and furthermore it seems very likely that the inspection team would find enough indications of a violation to keep an eye on the facility.

To ensure the routine character of the inspections, every party would be obliged to nominate at least one facility a year for inspection. The inspectorate would choose the objects of inspection at random from the nominated facilities. This implies that a facility that is nominated by many parties would have a large chance of being inspected. While the inspection protocol is in development, a start could be made with some trial inspections.

Conclusion

Twenty years ago, when the Biological Weapons Convention was negotiated, biological warfare was improbable. The development of biotechnology, however, and its spread over the world now place the option of acquiring a biological warfare capability—in the long run, at least—within the reach of every country. Unless the current trend is reversed, a growing number of countries will make use of this option.

Aside from the issue of yellow rain, biological weapons have not been used since the Biological Weapons Convention came into force. But the use of chemical weapons by Iraq does not bode well, now that such countries as Iraq are acquiring biological weapons or already have done so.

The technology used to produce biological weapons comes from institutes and companies in the developed countries, and these countries are therefore obliged to prevent or at least to complicate direct or unknowing involvement of such companies and institutes in the production of biological weapons. But such measures cannot in the long run

prevent countries from acquiring biological weapons because of the dual-purpose character of most of the relevant
technology. The knowledge and technology to protect humans against diseases is inextricably connected with the
knowledge and technology to use these diseases for hostile
purposes. And to prevent countries from acquiring medical
technology is not a long-term option.

The only way to prevent proliferation of biological
weapons is to ban these weapons altogether by a reinforce-
ment of the Biological Weapons Convention. The confidence-building measures agreed upon at the Second Review
Conference are a useful first step, but they require refine-
ment and elaboration. Obscure phrases such as "directly
related to the Convention" require clarification. And the
scope of the data exchange should be widened to encompass
all facilities that are working on protection against biological weapons and that contain relevant agents (an agreed list
or lists should specify these agents) or relevant equipment
(such as P3 or P4 containment).

But confidence-building measures alone will not remove
all doubts. A verification regime also is required. Such a
regime should consist of routine inspections of declared facilities and the possibility of challenge inspections. In its
present form the Biological Weapons Convention is unverifiable because all principal provisions are linked to a party's
intentions. But introducing objective criteria would be relatively simple, and such criteria could form the basis of an
effective verification regime.

Several useful lessons can be drawn from the negotiations on a Chemical Weapons Convention – for example,
with regard to protection of confidential information. It
should, however, be remembered that biological agents do
fundamentally differ from chemical agents – for example, in
the way they are reproduced. A verification regime for the
Biological Weapons Convention will therefore pose special
problems that might require new solutions. The former negotiations have shown that an effective regime for inspec-

tion of potential production facilities cannot be developed at the negotiating table in Geneva but requires direct dialogue with representatives of those facilities and trial runs.

Biological weapons trial inspections are therefore urgently called for. The real challenge of strengthening the convention is not in analyzing its shortcomings and in proposing amendments and additions, as done in this book, but in working the suggestions out in practice and in getting all parties to agree. Developing a verification regime, in particular, will require a lot of work.

Whether the Biological Weapons Convention can be made into a convincing and effective ban is not a question that can be solved in political or diplomatic discussion but only by trying to work out an effective regime and by trying to solve the practical problems that undoubtedly will arise. Declaring that the convention cannot be saved, without having really tried to do so, comes down to saying that it is not worth saving.

The Third Review Conference, which will be held in Geneva in September 1991, will have to review the functioning of both the convention and the confidence-building measures that were agreed upon at the Second Review Conference. It will have to face the fact that, in spite of the measures, the risk of biological warfare has increased rather than decreased. Apart from despair, the review conference has no other option than making further efforts to strengthen the convention.

Agreeing to the limited measures of the Second Review Conference was not very difficult, but parties will now be confronted with the question of whether they are really willing to be open about activities related to biological weapons defense. A credible verification regime will entail costs, both literally and in terms of openness, but an effective ban is worth it.

Most parties agree that a review conference cannot decide on amendments or on an additional verification protocol to the convention. It is very unlikely, anyway, that agreement could be reached on verification of the Biological

Weapons Convention before agreement is reached on a Chemical Weapons Convention. Such agreement might be reached at the end of 1991 or in 1992. The Third Review Conference could, and should, agree on strengthening and widening the existing confidence-building measures and initiate preparations and negotiations toward a verification protocol to make the ban on biological weapons comprehensive, worldwide, and effective.

Appendix A

THE GENEVA PROTOCOL OF 1925

Protocol for the Prohibition of the Use in War of Asphyxiating, Poisonous or Other Gases, and of Bacteriological Methods of Warfare

The Undersigned Plenipotentiaries, in the name of their respective Governments:

Whereas the use in war of asphyxiating, poisonous or other gases, and of all analogous liquids, materials or devices, has been justly condemned by the general opinion of the civilized world; and

Whereas the prohibition of such use has been declared in Treaties to which the majority of Powers of the World are Parties; and

To the end that this prohibition shall be universally accepted as a part of International Law, binding alike the conscience and the practice of nations:

Declare:

That the High Contracting Parties, so far as they are not already Parties to Treaties prohibiting such use, accept this prohibition, agree to extend this prohibition to the use of bacteriological methods of warfare and agree to be bound as between themselves according to the terms of this declaration.

The High Contracting Parties will exert every effort to induce other States to accede to the present Protocol. Such accession will be notified to the Government of the French Republic, and by the latter to all signatory and acceding Powers, and will take effect on the date of the notification by the Government of the French Republic.

The present Protocol, of which the French and English texts are both authentic, shall be ratified as soon as possible. It shall bear today's date.

The ratifications of the present Protocol shall be addressed to the Government of the French Republic, which will at once notify the deposit of such ratification to each of the signatory and acceding Powers.

The instruments of ratification of and of accession to the present Protocol will remain deposited in the archives of the Government of the French Republic.

The present Protocol will come into force for each signatory Power as from the date of deposit of its ratification, and, from that moment, each Power will be bound as regards other powers which have already deposited their ratifications.

IN WITNESS WHEREOF the Plenipotentiaries have signed the present Protocol.

DONE at Geneva in a single copy, this seventeenth day of June, One Thousand Nine Hundred and Twenty-Five.

Appendix B

Convention on the Prohibition of the Development, Production and Stockpiling of Bacteriological (Biological) and Toxin Weapons and on Their Destruction (1972)

The States Parties to this Convention,

Determined to act with a view to achieving effective progress towards general and complete disarmament, including the prohibition and elimination of all types of weapons of mass destruction, and convinced that the prohibition of the development, production and stockpiling of chemical and bacteriological (biological) weapons and their elimination, through effective measures, will facilitate the achievement of general and complete disarmament under strict and effective international control,

Recognizing the important significance of the Protocol for the Prohibition of the Use in War of Asphyxiating, Poisonous or Other Gases, and of Bacteriological Methods of Warfare signed at Geneva on 17 June 1925, and conscious also of the contribution which the said Protocol has already made, and continues to make, to mitigating the horrors of war,

Reaffirming their adherence to the principles and objectives of that Protocol and calling upon all States to comply with them,

Recalling that the General Assembly of the United Nations has repeatedly condemned all actions contrary to the principles and objectives of the Geneva Protocol of 17 June 1925,

Desiring to contribute to the strengthening of confidence be-

116

tween peoples and the general improvement of the international atmosphere,

Desiring also to contribute to the realization of the purposes and principles of the Charter of the United Nations,

Convinced of the importance and urgency of eliminating from the arsenals of States, through effective measures, such danger-ous weapons of mass destruction as those using chemical or bac-teriological (biological) agents,

Recognizing that an agreement on the prohibition of bacterio-logical (biological) and toxin weapons represents a first possible step towards the achievement of agreement on effective measures also for prohibition of the development, production and stockpil-ing of chemical weapons, and determined to continue negotiations to that end,

Determined, for the sake of all mankind, to exclude complete-ly the possibility of bacteriological (biological) agents and toxins being used as weapons,

Convinced that such use would be repugnant to the con-science of mankind and that no effort should be spared to mini-mize this risk,

Have agreed as follows:

Article I

Each State Party to this Convention undertakes never in any circumstances to develop, produce, stockpile or otherwise acquire or retain:

(*a*) Microbial or other biological agents, or toxins whatever their origin or method of production, of types and in quantities that have no justification for prophylactic, protective or other peaceful purposes;

(*b*) Weapons, equipment or means of delivery designed to use such agents or toxins for hostile purposes or in armed conflict.

Article II

Each State Party to this Convention undertakes to destroy, or to divert to peaceful purposes, as soon as possible but not later than nine months after the entry into force of the Convention, all agents, toxins, weapons, equipment and means of delivery specified in Article I of the Convention, which are in its possession or under its jurisdiction or control. In implementing the provisions of this article all necessary safety precautions shall be observed to protect populations and the environment.

Article III

Each State Party to this Convention undertakes not to transfer to any recipient whatsoever, directly or indirectly, and not in any way to assist, encourage, or induce any State, group of States or international organizations to manufacture or otherwise acquire any of the agents, toxins, weapons, equipment or means of delivery specified in article I of the Convention.

Article IV

Each State Party to this Convention shall, in accordance with its constitutional processes, take any necessary measures to prohibit and prevent development, production, stockpiling, acquisition or retention of the agents, toxins, weapons, equipment and means of delivery specified in article I of the Convention, within the territory of such States, under its jurisdiction or under its control anywhere.

Article V

The States Parties to this Convention undertake to consult one another and to co-operate in solving any problems which may arise in relation to the objective of, or in the application of the provisions of, this Convention. Consultations and co-operation pursuant to this article may also be undertaken through appropriate international procedures within the framework of the United Nations and in accordance with its Charter.

Article VI

1. Any State Party to this Convention which finds that any other State Party is acting in breach of obligations deriving from the provisions of this Convention may lodge a complaint with the Security Council of the United Nations. Such a complaint should

include all possible evidence confirming its validity as well as a request for its consideration by the Security Council.

2. Each State Party to this Convention undertakes to cooperate in carrying out any investigation which the Security Council may initiate, in accordance with the provisions of the Charter of the United Nations, on the basis of the complaint received by the Council. The Security Council shall inform the States Parties to the Convention of the results of the investigation.

Article VII

Each State Party to this Convention undertakes to provide or support assistance, in accordance with the Charter of the United Nations, to any Party to the Convention which so requests, if the Security Council decides that such Party has been exposed to danger as a result of violation of this Convention.

Article VIII

Nothing in this Convention shall be interpreted as in any way limiting or detracting from the obligations assumed by any State under the Protocol for the Prohibition of the Use in War of Asphyxiating, Poisonous or Other Gases, and of Bacteriological Methods of Warfare, signed at Geneva on 17 June 1925.

Article IX

Each State Party to this Convention affirms the recognized objective of effective prohibition of chemical weapons and, to this end, undertakes to continue negotiations in good faith with a view to reaching early agreement on effective measures for the prohibition of their development, production and stockpiling and for their destruction, and on appropriate measures concerning equipment and means of delivery specifically designed for the production or use of chemical agents for weapons purposes.

Article X

1. The States Parties to this Convention undertake to facilitate

and have the right to participate in the fullest possible exchange of equipment, materials and scientific and technological information for the use of bacteriological (biological) agents and toxins for peaceful purposes. Parties to this Convention in a position to do so shall also co-operate in contributing individually or together with other States or international organizations to the further development and application of scientific discoveries in the field of bacteriology (biology) for prevention of disease, or for other peaceful purposes.

2. This Convention shall be implemented in a manner designed to avoid hampering the economic or technological development of States Parties to the Convention or international co-operation in the field of peaceful bacteriological (biological) activities, including the international exchange of bacteriological (biological) agents and toxins and equipment for the processing, use or production of bacteriological (biological) agents and toxins for peaceful purposes in accordance with the provisions of this Convention.

Article XI

Any State Party may propose amendments to this Convention. Amendments shall enter into force for each State Party accepting the amendments upon their acceptance by a majority of the States Parties to this Convention and thereafter for each remaining State Party on the date of acceptance by it.

Article XII

Five years after the entry into force of this Convention, or earlier if it is requested by a majority of Parties to the Convention by submitting a proposal to this effect to the Depositary Governments, a conference of States Parties to the Convention shall be held at Geneva, Switzerland, to review the operation of this Convention, with a view to assuring that the purposes of the preamble and the provisions of the Convention, including the provisions concerning negotiations on chemical weapons, are being realized. Such review shall take into account any new scientific and technological developments relevant to this Convention.

Article XIII

1. This Convention shall be of unlimited duration.

2. Each State Party to this Convention shall, in exercising its national sovereignty, have the right to withdraw from the Convention if it decides that extraordinary events, related to the subject matter of this Convention, have jeopardized the supreme interests of its country. It shall give notice of such withdrawal to all other States Parties to the Convention and to the United Nations Security Council three months in advance. Such notice shall include a statement of the extraordinary events it regards as having jeopardized its supreme interests.

Article XIV

1. This Convention shall be open to all States for signature. Any State which does not sign the Convention before its entry into force in accordance with paragraph 3 of this article may accede to it any time.

2. This Convention shall be subject to ratification by signatory States. Instruments of ratification and instruments of accession shall be deposited with the Governments of the Union of Soviet Socialist Republics, the United Kingdom of Great Britain and Northern Ireland and the United States of America, which are hereby designated the Depositary Governments.

3. This Convention shall enter into force after the deposit of the instruments of ratification by twenty-two Governments, including the Governments designated as Depositaries of the Convention.

4. For States whose instruments of ratification or accession are deposited subsequent to the entry into force of this Convention, it shall enter into force on the date of the deposit of their instruments of ratification or accession.

5. The Depositary Governments shall promptly inform all signatory and acceding States of the date of each signature, the date of deposit of each instrument of ratification or of accession and the date of the entry into force of this Convention, and of the receipt of other notices.

6. This Convention shall be registered by the Depositary Governments pursuant to Article 102 of the Charter of the United Nations.

Article XV

This Convention, the Chinese, English, French, Russian and Spanish texts of which are equally authentic, shall be deposited in the archives of the Depositary Governments. Duly certified copies of this Convention shall be transmitted by the Depositary Governments to the Governments of the signatory and acceding States.

In witness whereof the undersigned, duly authorized, have signed this Convention.

Appendix C

Final Declaration of the First Review Conference of the Parties to the Convention on the Prohibition of the Development, Production and Stockpiling of Bacteriological (Biological) and Toxin Weapons and on Their Destruction

The States Parties to the Convention on the Prohibition of the Development, Production and Stockpiling of Bacteriological (Biological) and Toxin Weapons and on Their Destruction, having met in Geneva 3–21 March 1980 under the provisions of Article XII to review the operation of the Convention with a view to assuring that the purposes of the preamble and the provisions of the Convention are being realized:

Reaffirming their determination to act with a view to achieving effective progress towards general and complete disarmament including the prohibition and elimination of all types of weapons of mass destruction and convinced that the prohibition of the development, production and stockpiling of chemical and bacteriological (biological) weapons and their elimination, through effective measures, will facilitate the achievement of general and complete disarmament under strict and effective international control,

Recognizing the continuing importance of the Convention and its objectives and the common interest of mankind in the elimination of bacteriological (biological) and toxin weapons,

Affirming their belief that universal adherence to the Convention would enhance international peace and security, would not hamper economic or technological development, and further, would facilitate the wider exchange of information for the use of bacteriological (biological) agents for peaceful purposes,

Reaffirming their adherence to the principle and objectives of the Geneva Protocol of 17 June 1925 and calling upon all States to comply strictly with them,

Recalling that the General Assembly of the United Nations has repeatedly condemned all actions contrary to the said principles and objectives,

Recognizing the importance of achieving international agreement on effective measures for the prohibition of the development, production and stockpiling of chemical weapons and for their destruction as a matter of high priority,

Noting the relevant provisions of the Final Document of the Tenth Special Session of the General Assembly devoted to Disarmament,

Appealing to all States to refrain from any action which might place the Convention or any of its provisions in jeopardy,

Declare as follows:

The States Parties to the Convention reaffirm their strong determination for the sake of all mankind, to exclude completely the possibility of bacteriological (biological) agents and toxins being used as weapons. They reaffirm their strong support for the Convention, their continued dedication to its principles and objectives and their commitment to implement effectively its provisions.

Article I

The Conference notes the importance of Article I as the Article which defines the scope of the Convention and reaffirms its support for the provisions of this Article.

The Conference believes that Article I has proved sufficiently comprehensive to have covered recent scientific and technological developments relevant to the Convention.

Article II

The Conference notes the importance of Article II and emphasizes that States which become Parties to the Convention, in implementing the provisions of this Article, shall observe all necessary safety precautions to protect populations and the environment.

The Conference welcomes the declarations of several States Parties to the effect either that they do not possess and have never possessed agents, toxins, weapons, equipment or means of delivery specified in Article I of the Convention, or that having possessed them they have destroyed them or diverted them to peaceful purposes. The Conference believes that such voluntary declarations contribute to increased confidence in the Convention and believes that States not having made such voluntary declarations should do so.

Article III

The Conference notes the importance of the provisions of Article III which prescribes the transfer of agents, toxins, weapons, equipment or means of delivery specified in Article I of the Convention to any recipient whatsoever and the furnishing of assistance, encouragement or inducement to any State, group of States or international organizations to manufacture or otherwise acquire them.

Article IV

The Conference notes the provisions of Article IV, which requires each State Party to take any necessary measures to prohibit and prevent the development, production, stockpiling, acquisition or retention of the agents, toxins, weapons, equipment and means of delivery specified in Article I of the Convention, within its territory, under its jurisdiction or under its control anywhere, and calls upon all States Parties which have not yet taken any necessary measures in accordance with their constitutional processes to do so immediately.

The Conference invites States Parties which have found it necessary to enact specific legislation or take other regulatory measures relevant to this Article to make available the appropriate texts to the United Nations Centre for Disarmament, for the purposes of consultation.

Article V

The Conference notes the importance of Article V which contains the undertaking of States Parties to consult one another and to co-operate in solving any problems which may arise in relation to the objective of, or in the application of the provisions of, the Convention.

The Conference considers that the flexibility of the provisions concerning consultations and co-operation on any problems which may arise in relation to the objective, or in the application of the provisions of, the Convention, enables interested States Parties to use various international procedures which would make it possible to ensure effectively and adequately the implementation of the Convention provisions taking into account the concern expressed by the Conference participants to this effect.

These procedures include, *inter alia*, the rights of any State Party subsequently to request that a consultative meeting open to all States Parties be convened at expert level.

The Conference, noting the concerns and differing views expressed on the adequacy of Article V, believes that this question should be further considered at an appropriate time.

Article VI

The Conference also notes the importance of Article VI, which in addition to the procedures contained in Article V, provides for any State Party, which finds that any other State Party is acting in breach of its obligations under the Convention, to lodge a complaint with the United Nations Security Council, and under which each State Party undertakes to co-operate in carrying out any investigation which the Security Council may initiate.

The Conference further notes that no State Party has invoked these provisions.

Article VII

The Conference notes with satisfaction that it has not proved necessary to invoke the provisions of Article VII.

Article VIII

The Conference reaffirms that nothing contained in the Convention shall be interpreted as in any way limiting or detracting from the obligations assumed by any State under the Protocol for the prohibition of the use in war of asphyxiating, poisonous or other gases and of bacteriological methods of warfare, signed at Geneva on 17 June 1925. The conference calls on those States Parties to the Convention which are Parties to the Protocol to comply strictly with its provisions and those States not yet Parties to the said Protocol to ratify or accede to it at the earliest possible date.

Article IX

The Conference notes the importance of the provisions of Article IX and of the preambular paragraphs concerning the commitment of States Parties to continue negotiations in good faith with a view to reaching early agreement on effective measures for the prohibition of the development, production and stockpiling of chemical weapons and for their destruction. The Conference deeply regrets that such agreement has not yet become a reality despite the fact that eight years have already elapsed since the Convention was opened for signature.

The Conference urges the Committee on Disarmament to undertake negotiations on an agreement on the complete and effective prohibition of the development, production and stockpiling of all chemical weapons and on their destruction, as a matter of high priority, taking into account all existing proposals and future initiatives. To this end, the Conference welcomes the establishment, by the Committee on Disarmament, of an *ad hoc* working group on chemical weapons and urges all the members of the Committee to contribute towards the fulfillment of its mandate.

The Conference takes note of the bilateral USA-USSR report (CD/48) presented to the Committee on Disarmament on the progress of their negotiations undertaken with a view to presenting a joint initiative to that Committee and notes their stated intention to continue intensive negotiations to this end.

The Conference reaffirms the obligation assumed by States Parties to the Convention to continue negotiations in good faith towards the recognized objectives of an early agreement on complete, effective and adequately verifiable measures for the prohibition of the development, production and stockpiling of chemical weapons and for their destruction.

Article X

The Conference notes that since the entry into force of the Convention, increasing importance has been attached by the international community to the principle that the disarmament process should help promote economic and social development, particularly in the developing countries. Accordingly, the Conference calls upon States Parties, especially developed countries, to increase, individually, or together with other States or international organizations, their scientific and technological co-operation, particularly with developing countries, in the peaceful uses of bacteriological (biological) agents and toxins. Such co-operation should include, *inter alia*, the transfer and exchange of information, training of personnel and transfer of materials and equipment on a more systematic and long-term basis.

Furthermore, the Conference notes with satisfaction that the implementation of the Convention has not hampered the economic or technological development of States Parties.

The Conference requests the United Nations Secretariat to include in the background materials prepared for the second Review Conference of the Parties to the Convention on the Prohibition of the Development, Production and Stockpiling of Bacteriological (Biological) and Toxin Weapons and on Their Destruction, information on the implementation of Article X by States Parties.

Article XI

The Conference notes the importance of the provisions of Article XI and that during the first five years of the operation of the Convention these provisions have not been invoked.

Article XII

The Conference welcomes the spirit of co-operation in which this Review Conference was conducted, and believes that such conferences constitute an effective method of reviewing the operation of the Convention with a view to ensuring that its purposes and provisions are being realized, in particular with respect to any new scientific and technological developments relevant to the Convention.

The Conference decides that a second Review Conference shall be held in Geneva at the request of a majority of States Parties not earlier than 1985 and, in any case, not later than 1990.

Any information provided by States Parties on scientific and technological developments relevant to the Convention, and on its implementation, shall be made available periodically to States Parties, in particular through the United Nations Centre for Disarmament.

Article XIII

The Conference notes the provisions of Article XIII and expresses its satisfaction that no State Party to the Convention has exercised its right to withdraw from the Convention.

Article XIV

The Conference notes with satisfaction that 81 States have ratified the Convention, 6 States have acceded to the Convention and a further 37 States have signed but have yet to ratify the Convention. The Conference calls upon all signatory States which have not ratified the Convention to do so without delay and upon those States which have not signed the Convention to join the States Parties thereto in the efforts to eliminate the risk of biological warfare.

Article XV

The Conference notes the provisions of Article XV.

Appendix D

Final Declaration of the Second Review Conference of the Parties to the Convention on the Prohibition of the Development, Production and Stockpiling of Bacteriological (Biological) and Toxin Weapons and on Their Destruction

Preamble

The States Parties to the Convention on the Prohibition of the Development, Production and Stockpiling of Bacteriological (Biological) and Toxin Weapons and on Their Destruction, having met in Geneva 8–26 September 1986 in accordance with a decision by the First Review Conference 1980 and at the request of a majority of States Parties to the Convention, to review the operation of the Convention with a view to assuring that the purposes of the Preamble and the provisions of the Convention are being realized:

Reaffirming their determination to act with a view to achieving effective progress towards general and complete disarmament, including the prohibition and elimination of all types of weapons of mass destruction, and convinced that the prohibition of the development, production and stockpiling of chemical and bacteriological (biological) weapons and their elimination, through effective measures, will facilitate the achievement of general and complete disarmament under strict and effective international control,

Recognizing the continuing importance of the Convention and its objectives and the common interest of mankind in the elimination of bacteriological (biological) and toxin weapons,

Affirming their belief that universal adherence to the Convention would enhance international peace and security, would not hamper economic or technological development and, further, would facilitate the wider exchange of information for the use of bacteriological (biological) agents for peaceful purposes,

Confirming the common interest in strengthening the authority and the effectiveness of the Convention, to promote confidence and co-operation among States Parties,

Affirming the importance of strengthening international co-operation in the field of biotechnology, genetic engineering, microbiology and other related areas,

Reaffirming their adherence to the principles and objectives of the Geneva Protocol of 17 June 1925 and calling upon all States to comply strictly with them,

Recalling that the General Assembly of the United Nations has repeatedly condemned all actions contrary to the said principles and objectives,

Recognizing the importance of achieving as a matter of high priority an international convention on the complete and effective prohibition of the development, production and stockpiling of chemical weapons and on their destruction,

Noting the relevant provisions of the Final Document of the first special session of the General Assembly devoted to disarmament,

Appealing to all States to refrain from any action which might place the Convention or any of its provisions in jeopardy,

Declare their strong determination, for the sake of all mankind, to exclude completely the possibility of microbial, or other biological agents, or toxins being used as weapons and reaffirm their strong support for the Convention, their continued dedication to its principles and objectives and their legal obligation under international law to implement and strictly comply with its provisions.

Article I

The Conference notes the importance of Article I as the Article which defines the scope of the Convention and reaffirms its support for the provisions of this Article.

The Conference concludes that the scope of Article I covers scientific and technological developments relevant to the Convention.

The Conference notes statements by some States Parties that compliance with Articles I, II and III was, in their view, subject to grave doubt in some cases and that efforts to resolve those concerns had not been successful. The Conference notes the statements by other States Parties that such a doubt was unfounded and, in their view, not in accordance with the Convention. The Conference agrees that the application by States Parties of a positive approach in questions of compliance in accordance with the provisions of the Convention was in the interest of all States Parties and that this would serve to promote confidence among States Parties.

The Conference, conscious of apprehensions arising from relevant scientific and technological developments, *inter alia*, in the fields of microbiology, genetic engineering and biotechnology, and the possibilities of their use for purposes inconsistent with the objectives and the provisions of the Convention, reaffirms that the undertaking given by the States Parties in Article I applies to all such developments.

The Conference reaffirms that the Convention unequivocally applies to all natural or artificially created microbial or other biological agents or toxins whatever their origin or method of production. Consequently, toxins (both proteinaceous and non-proteinaceous) of a microbial, animal or vegetable nature and their synthetically produced analogues are covered.

Article II

The Conference notes the importance of Article II and welcomes the statements made by States which have become Parties to the Convention since the First Review Conference that they do not possess agents, toxins, weapons, equipment or means of delivery referred to in Article I of the Convention. The Conference believes that such statements enhance confidence in the Convention.

The Conference stresses that States which become Parties to the Convention, in implementing the provisions of this Article, shall observe all necessary safety precautions to protect populations and the environment.

Article III

The Conference notes the importance of Article III and welcomes the statements which States that have acceded to the Convention have made to the effect that they have not transferred agents, toxins, weapons, equipment or means of delivery, specified in Article I of the Convention, to any recipient whatsoever and have not furnished assistance, encouragement or inducement to any State, group of States or international organizations to manufacture or otherwise acquire them. The Conference affirms that Article III is sufficiently comprehensive so as to cover any recipient whatsoever at international, national or sub-national levels.

The Conference notes that the provisions of this Article should not be used to impose restrictions and/or limitations on the transfer for purposes consistent with the objectives and the provisions of the Convention of scientific knowledge, technology, equipment and materials to States Parties.

Article IV

The Conference notes the importance of Article IV, under which each State Party shall, in accordance with its constitutional processes, take any necessary measures to prohibit or prevent any acts or actions which would contravene the Convention.

The Conference calls upon all States Parties which have not yet taken any necessary measures in accordance with their constitutional processes, as required by the Article, to do so immediately.

The Conference notes that States Parties, as requested by the First Review Conference, have provided to the United Nations Department for Disarmament Affairs information on and the texts of specific legislation enacted or other regulatory measures taken by them, relevant to this Article. The Conference invites States Parties to continue to provide such information and texts to the United Nations Department for Disarmament Affairs for purposes of consultation.

The Conference notes the importance of

- legislative, administrative and other measures designed effectively to guarantee compliance with the provisions of the Convention within the territory under the jurisdiction or control of a State Party;
- legislation regarding the physical protection of laboratories and facilities to prevent unauthorized access to and removal of pathogenic or toxin material; and
- inclusion in textbooks and in medical, scientific and military educational programmes of information dealing with the prohibition of bacteriological (biological) and toxin weapons and the provisions of the Geneva Protocol

and believes that such measures which States might undertake in accordance with their constitutional process would strengthen the effectiveness of the Convention.

Article V

The Conference notes the importance of Article V and reaffirms the obligation assumed by States Parties to consult and co-operate with one another in solving any problems which may arise in relation to the objective of, or in the application of the provisions of, the Convention.

The Conference reaffirms that consultation and co-operation pursuant to this Article may also be undertaken through appropriate international procedures within the framework of the United Nations and in accordance with its Charter.

The Conference confirms the conclusion in the Final Declaration of the First Review Conference that these procedures include, *inter alia*, the right of any State Party to request that a consultative meeting open to all States Parties be convened at expert level.

The Conference stresses the need for all States to deal seriously with compliance issues and emphasizes that the failure to do so undermines the Convention and the arms control process in general.

The Conference appeals to States Parties to make all possible efforts to solve any problems which may arise in relation to the objective of, or in the application of the provisions of, the Convention with a view towards encouraging strict observance of the provisions subscribed to. The Conference further requests that information on such efforts be provided to the Third Review Conference.

The Conference, taking into account views expressed concerning the need to strengthen the implementation of the provisions of Article V, has agreed:

- that a consultative meeting shall be promptly convened when requested by a State Party;
- that a consultative meeting may consider any problems which may arise in relation to the objective of, or in the application of the provisions of the Convention, suggest ways and means for further clarifying, *inter alia*, with assistance of technical experts, any matter considered ambiguous or unresolved, as well as initiate appropriate international procedures within the framework of the United Nations and in accordance with its Charter;
- that the consultative meeting, or any State Party, may request specialized assistance in solving any problems which may arise in relation to the objective of, or in the application of the provisions of, the Convention, through, *inter alia*, appropriate international procedures within the framework of the United Nations and in accordance with its Charter;
- the Conference considers that States Parties shall co-operate with the consultative meeting in its consideration of any problems which may arise in relation to the objective of, or in the application of the provisions of the Convention, and in clarifying ambiguous and unresolved matters, as well as co-operate in appropriate international procedures within the framework of the United Nations and in accordance with its Charter.

The Conference, mindful of the provisions of Article V and Article X, and determined to strengthen the authority of the Convention and to enhance confidence in the implementation of its provisions, agrees that the States Parties are to implement, on the basis of mutual co-operation, the following measures, in order to prevent or reduce the occurrence of ambiguities, doubts and suspicions, and in order to improve international co-operation in the field of peaceful bacteriological (biological) activities:

1. Exchange of data, including name, location, scope and general description of activities, on research centres and laboratories that meet very high national or international safety standards established for handling, for permitted purposes, biological materials that pose a high individual and community risk or specialize in permitted biological activities directly related to the Convention.
2. Exchange of information on all outbreaks of infectious diseases and similar occurrences caused by toxins that seem to deviate from the normal pattern as regards type, development, place, or time of occurrence. If possible, the information provided would include, as soon as it is available, data on the type of disease, approximate area affected, and number of cases.
3. Encouragement of publication of results of biological research directly related to the Convention, in scientific journals generally available to States Parties, as well as promotion of use for permitted purposes of knowledge gained in this research.
4. Active promotion of contacts between scientists engaged in biological research directly related to the Convention, including exchanges for joint research on a mutually agreed basis.

The Conference decides to hold an ad hoc meeting of scientific and technical experts from States Parties to finalize the modalities for the exchange of information and data by working out, *inter alia*, appropriate forms to be used by States Parties for the exchange of information agreed to in this Final Declaration, thus enabling States Parties to follow a standardized procedure. The group shall meet in Geneva for the period 31 March–5 April 1987 and shall communicate the results of the work to the States Parties immediately thereafter.

Pending the results of this meeting, the Conference urges States Parties to promptly apply these measures and report the data agreed upon to the United Nations Department for Disarmament Affairs.

The Conference requests the United Nations Department for Disarmament Affairs to make available the information received to all States Parties.

Article VI

The Conference also notes the importance of Article VI, which in addition to the procedures contained in Article V, provides for any State Party, which finds that any other State Party is acting in breach of its obligations under the Convention, to lodge a complaint with the United Nations Security Council and under which each State Party undertakes to co-operate in carrying out any investigation which the Security Council may initiate.

The Conference notes the need to further improve and strengthen this and other procedures to enhance greater confidence in the Convention. The Conference considers that the Security Council may, if it deems it necessary, request the advice of the World Health Organization in carrying out any investigation of complaints lodged with the Council.

Article VII

The Conference notes that these provisions have not been invoked.

Article VIII

The Conference reaffirms the importance of Article VIII and stresses the importance of the Protocol for the Prohibition of the Use in War of Asphyxiating, Poisonous or Other Gases and of Bacteriological Methods of Warfare.

The Conference reaffirms that nothing contained in the Convention shall be interpreted as in any way limiting or detracting from the obligations assumed by any State under the Protocol for the Prohibition of the Use in War of Asphyxiating, Poisonous or Other Gases and of Bacteriological Methods of Warfare, signed at Geneva on 17 June 1925. Noting the report of the Security Council (S/17911), the Conference appeals to all States Parties to the Geneva Protocol of 1925 to fulfill their obligations assumed under that Protocol and urges all States not yet Parties to the said Protocol to adhere to it at the earliest possible date.

Article IX

The Conference reaffirms the obligation assumed by States Parties to continue negotiations in good faith towards an early agreement on effective measures for the prohibition of the development, production and stockpiling of chemical weapons and for their destruction.

All States Parties participating in the Conference reiterate their strong commitment to this important goal.

The Conference notes with satisfaction the substantial progress made in the negotiations on a convention on the prohibition of chemical weapons in the Conference on Disarmament during the period under review. The Conference also takes note of the bilateral talks between the Union of Soviet Socialist Republics and the United States of America on all aspects of the prohibition of chemical weapons.

The Conference nevertheless deeply regrets that an agreement on a convention on chemical weapons has not yet been reached.

The Conference urges the Conference on Disarmament to exert all possible efforts to conclude an agreement on a total ban of chemical weapons with effective verification provisions by the earliest possible date.

Article X

The Conference emphasizes the increasing importance of the provisions of Article X, especially in the light of recent scientific and technological developments in the field of biotechnology, bacteriological (biological) agents and toxins with peaceful applications, which have vastly increased the potential for co-operation between States to help promote economic and social development, and scientific and technological progress, particularly in the developing countries, in conformity with their interests, needs and priorities.

The Conference, while acknowledging what has already been done towards this end, notes with concern the increasing gap between the developed and the developing countries in the field of biotechnology, genetic engineering, microbiology and other related areas. The Conference accordingly urges States Parties to provide wider access to and share their scientific and technological knowledge in this field, on an equal and non-discriminatory basis, in particular with developing countries, for the benefit of all mankind.

The Conference urges that States Parties take specific measures within their competence for the promotion of the fullest possible international co-operation in this field through their active intervention. Such measures could include, *inter alia*:

- transfer and exchange of information concerning research programmes in bio-sciences;
- wider transfer and exchange of information, materials and equipment among States on a systematic and long-term basis;
- active promotion of contacts between scientists and technical personnel on a reciprocal basis, in relevant fields;
- increased technical co-operation, including training opportunities to developing countries in the use of bio-sciences and genetic engineering for peaceful purposes;
- facilitating the conclusion of bilateral, regional and multiregional agreements providing on a mutually advantageous, equal and non-discriminatory basis, for their participation in the development and application of biotechnology;
- encouraging the co-ordination of national and regional programmes and working out in an appropriate manner the ways and means of co-operation in this field.

The Conference calls for greater co-operation in international public health and disease control.

The Conference urges that co-operation under Article X should be actively pursued within the bilateral and the multilateral framework and further urges the use of existing institutional means within the United Nations system and the full utilization of the possibilities provided by the specialized agencies and other international organizations.

The Conference, noting that co-operation would be best initiated by improved institutionalized direction and co-ordination, recommends that measures to ensure co-operation on such a basis be pursued within the existing means of the United Nations system. Accordingly, the Conference requests the Secretary-General of the United Nations to propose for inclusion on the agenda of a relevant United Nations body a discussion and examination of the means for improving institutional mechanisms in order to facilitate the fullest possible exchange of equipment, materials and scientific and technological information for the use of bacteriological (biological) agents and toxins for peaceful purposes. The Conference recommends that invitations to participate in this discussion and examination should be extended to all States Parties, whether or not they are members of the United Nations and concerned specialized agencies.

The Conference requests the States Parties and the United Nations Secretariat to include in the document materials prepared for the above-mentioned discussion of States Parties, information and suggestions on the implementation of Article X, taking into account the preceding paragraphs. Furthermore, it urges the specialized agencies, *inter alia*, FAO, WHO, UNESCO, WIPO, and UNIDO, to participate in this discussion and fully cooperate with the Secretary-General of the United Nations and requests the Secretary-General to send all relevant information of this Conference to these agencies.

The Conference, referring to paragraph 35 of the Final Document of the first special session of the General Assembly devoted to disarmament, stresses the importance of the obligations under Article X in promoting economic and social development of developing countries, particularly in the light of the United Nations Conference on the Relationship between Disarmament and Development, for the States participating therein, scheduled for 1987.

The Conference, to ensure compliance with Article X, also requests States Parties and the United Nations Secretariat to provide information relevant to the implementation of the Article for examination by the next conference of States Parties.

The Conference upholds that the above-mentioned measures would positively strengthen the Convention.

Article XI

The Conference notes the importance of Article XI and that since the entry into force of the Convention the provisions of the Article have not been invoked.

Article XII

The Conference decides that a Third Review Conference shall be held in Geneva at the request of a majority of States Parties not later than 1991.

The Conference, noting the differing views with regard to verification, decides that the Third Review Conference shall consider, *inter alia*:

- the impact of scientific and technological developments relevant to the Convention;
- the relevance for effective implementation of the Convention of the results achieved in the negotiations on prohibition of chemical weapons;
- the effectiveness of the provisions in Article V for consultation and co-operation and of the co-operative measures agreed in this Final Declaration; and
- in the light of these considerations and of the provisions of Article XI, whether or not further actions are called for to create further co-operative measures in the context of Article V, or legally binding improvements to the Convention, or a combination of both.

Article XIII

The Conference notes the provisions of Article XIII and expresses its satisfaction that no State Party to the Convention has exercised its right to withdraw from the Convention.

Article XIV

The Conference notes with satisfaction that a significant number of States have ratified or acceded to the Convention since the First Review Conference and that there are now more than 100 States Parties to the Convention, including all the permanent Members of the Security Council of the United Nations.

The Conference calls upon States which have not yet ratified or acceded to the Convention to do so without delay and upon those States which have not signed the Convention to join the

States Parties thereto thus contributing to the achievement of universal adherence to the Convention.

The Conference makes an urgent appeal to all States Parties to the Convention on the Prohibition of the Development, Production and Stockpiling of Bacteriological (Biological) and Toxin Weapons and on Their Destruction, which did not participate in its work, to give their effective co-operation and take part more actively in the common endeavour of all the Contracting Parties to strengthen the objectives and purposes of the Convention. In this connection, the Conference urges all States Parties that were absent to take part in the future work envisaged in this Final Declaration.

Article XV

The Conference notes the provisions of Article XV.

The following proposals were submitted to the Conference and considered by it; their full text is reproduced in the Final Document of the Review Conference.

Appendix E

Modalities for the Exchange of Information, from the Report of the Ad Hoc meeting of Scientific and Technical Experts from States Parties to the Convention on the Prohibition of the Development, Production and Stockpiling of Bacteriological (Biological) and Toxin Weapons and on Their Destruction (chap. 2 of BWC/CONF.II/EX/2)

A. Exchange of data on research centres and laboratories

At the Second Review Conference it was agreed that States Parties are to implement the following:

> Exchange of data, including name, location, scope and general description of activities, on research centres and laboratories that meet very high national or international safety standards established for handling, for permitted purposes, biological materials that pose a high individual and community risk or specialize in permitted biological activities directly related to the Convention.

Modalities

The *Ad Hoc* Meeting agreed that data should be provided on each research centre or laboratory, within the territory of a State Party, under its jurisdiction or under its control anywhere,

(a) which has maximum containment unit(s) meeting the criteria for a "maximum containment laboratory" as specified in the 1983 WHO Laboratory Biosafety Manual (Annex IV), such as those designated as Biosafety Level 4 (BL4) or P4, or equivalent standard; or

(b) which has containment unit(s) and specializes in research or development for prophylactic or protective purposes against possible hostile use of microbial and/or other biological agents or toxins.

To enable the States Parties to follow a standardized procedure, the *Ad Hoc* Meeting has agreed that Form 1 should be used for the exchange of data on research centres and laboratories.

<u>Form 1</u>

Exchange of data on research centres and laboratories

1. Name(s) of the research
   centre and/or laboratory   _____

2. Responsible public or private
   organization or company   _____

3. Location and postal address   _____
                                     _____
                                     _____
                                     _____

4. Source(s) of financing of the reported activity, including indication if the activity is wholly or partly financed by the Ministry
   of Defence

   _____

5. Number of maximum containment units* within the research
   centre and/or laboratory, with an indication of their respective
   size (m^2)

   _____

6. If no maximum containment unit, indicate highest level of
   protection

   _____

7. Scope and general description of activities, including type(s) of
   micro-organisms and/or toxins as appropriate

   _____

   _____

   _____

---

*In accordance with the 1983 WHO Laboratory Biosafety Manual,
or equivalent.

B. Exchange of information on outbreaks of infectious diseases and similar occurrences caused by toxins

At the Second Review Conference it was agreed that States Parties are to implement the following:

> Exchange of information on all outbreaks of infectious diseases and similar occurrences caused by toxins that seem to deviate from the normal pattern as regards type, development, place, or time of occurrence. If possible, the information provided would include, as soon as it is available, data on the type of disease, approximate area affected, and number of cases.

Modalities

In its discussion of what constitutes an outbreak the *Ad Hoc* Meeting consulted an expert from the World Health Organization who informed that the WHO considers the terms "outbreak" and "epidemic" to be interchangeable, and the following definition was suggested:

> An outbreak or epidemic is the occurrence of an unusually large or unexpected number of cases of an illness or health-related event in a given place at a given time. The number of cases considered as unusual will vary according to the illness or event and the community concerned.

Furthermore, reference was made to the following definitions:

— An *epidemic* of infectious disease is defined as the occurrence of an unusually large or unexpected number of cases of a disease known or suspected to be of infectious origin, for a given place and time. It is usually a rapidly evolving situation, requiring a rapid response. (WHO internal document CDS/Mtg/82.1)

— The occurrence in a community or region of cases of an illness, specific health-related behaviour, or other health-related events clearly in excess of normal expectancy. The community or region, and the time period in which the cases occur, are specified precisely. The number of cases indicating the presence of an epidemic will vary according to the agent, size and type of population exposed, previous experience or lack of exposure to the disease, and time and place of occurrence: epidemicity is thus relative to usual frequency of the disease in the same area, among the specified population, at the same season of the year. A single case of a communicable disease long absent from a population or first invasion by a disease not previously recognized in that area requires immediate reporting and full field investigation: two cases of such a disease associated in time and place may be sufficient evidence to be considered an epidemic. (Last, J.M., *A Dictionary of Epidemiology*, Oxford University Press, New York, Oxford, Toronto, 1983)

The *Ad Hoc* Meeting agreed on the following:

1. In determining what constitutes an outbreak States Parties are recommended to take guidance from the above.

2. Since no universal standards exist for what might constitute a deviation from the normal pattern, States Parties are encouraged

- to fully utilize existing reporting systems within the WHO, and
- to provide background information on diseases caused by organisms which meet the criteria for risk groups III and IV according to the classification in the 1983 WHO Laboratory Biosafety Manual, the occurrence of which, in their respective areas, does not necessarily constitute a deviation from normal patterns.*

3. Exchange of data on outbreaks that seem to deviate from the normal pattern is considered particularly important in the following cases:

- when the cause of the outbreak cannot be readily determined or the causative agent** is difficult to diagnose,
- when the disease may be caused by organisms which meet the criteria for risk group III or IV, according to the classification in 1983 WHO Laboratory Biosafety Manual,
- when the causative agent is exotic to a given region,

---

*This information should be provided in accordance with E.1.

**It is understood that this may include organisms made pathogenic by molecular techniques, such as genetic engineering.

- when the disease follows an unusual pattern of development,
- when the disease occurs in the vicinity of research centres and laboratories subject to exchange of data under item A,
- when suspicions arise of the possible occurrence of a new disease.

4. In order to enhance confidence, an initial report of an outbreak of an infectious disease or a similar occurrence that deviates from the normal pattern should be given promptly after cognizance of the outbreak and should be followed up by annual reports.

To enable States Parties to follow a standardized procedure, the *Ad Hoc* Meeting has agreed that Form 2 should be used, to the extent information is known and/or applicable, for the exchange of initial as well as annual information.

5. In order to improve international co-operation in the field of peaceful bacteriological (biological) activities and in order to prevent or reduce the occurrence of ambiguities, doubts and suspicions, States Parties are encouraged to invite experts from other States Parties to assist in the handling of an outbreak, and to respond favourably to such invitations.

<u>Form 2</u>

*Information on outbreaks of infectious diseases and similar
occurrences that seem to deviate from the normal pattern*

1. Time of cognizance of the
   outbreak _____
2. Location and approximate
   area affected _____
3. Type of disease/intoxication _____
4. Suspected source of disease/
   intoxication _____
5. Possible causative agent(s) _____
6. Main characteristics of
   systems _____
7. Detailed symptoms, when
   applicable _____
   - respiratory _____
   - circulatory _____
   - neurological/behavioral _____
   - intestinal _____
   - dermatological _____
   - nephrological _____
   - other _____
8. Deviation(s) from the normal
   pattern as regards _____
   - type _____
   - development _____
   - place of occurrence _____
   - time of occurrence _____
   - symptoms _____
   - virulence pattern _____
   - drug resistance pattern _____
   - agent(s) difficult to
     diagnose _____
   - presence of unusual
     vectors _____
   - other _____
9. Approximate number of
   primary cases _____

10. Approximate number of total
    cases   _____
11. Number of deaths   _____
12. Development of the outbreak   _____
13. Measures taken   _____

*C. Encouragement of publication of results and
promotion of use of knowledge*

At the Second Review Conference it was agreed that States Parties are to implement the following:

> Encouragement of publication of results of biological research directly related to the Convention, in scientific journals generally available to States Parties, as well as promotion of use for permitted purposes of knowledge gained in this research.

Modalities

The *Ad Hoc* Meeting agreed on the following:

1. It is recommended that basic research in biosciences, and particularly that directly related to the Convention should generally be unclassified and that applied research to the extent possible, without infringing on national and commercial interests, should also be unclassified.

2. States parties are encouraged to provide information on their policy as regards publication of results of biological research, indicating, *inter alia*, their policies as regards publication of results of research carried out in research centres and laboratories subject to exchange of information under item A and publication of research on outbreaks of diseases covered by item B, and to provide information on relevant scientific journals and other relevant scientific publications generally available to States Parties.

3. The *Ad Hoc* Meeting discussed the question of co-operation and assistance as regards the safe handling of biological material covered by the Convention. It concluded that other international fora were engaged in this field and expressed its support for efforts aimed at enhancing such co-operation.

D. Active promotion of contacts

At the Second Review Conference it was agreed that States Parties are to implement the following:

> Active promotion of contacts between scientists engaged in biological research directly related to the Convention, including exchanges for joint research on a mutually agreed basis.

Modalities

The *Ad Hoc* Meeting agreed on the following:

In order to actively promote professional contacts between scientists, joint research projects and other activities aimed at preventing or reducing the occurrence of ambiguities, doubts and suspicions and at improving international co-operation in the field of peaceful bacteriological (biological) activities, States Parties are encouraged to provide information, to the extent possible,

- — on planned international conferences, seminars, symposia and similar events dealing with biological research directly related to the Convention,
- — on other opportunities for exchange of scientists, joint research or other measures to promote contacts between scientists engaged in biological research directly related to the Convention.

To enable States Parties to follow a standardized procedure, the *Ad Hoc* Meeting has agreed that Form 3 should be used for exchange of information under this item.

E. Procedural modalities

1. Bearing in mind resolution 41/58 A, adopted on 3 December 1986 by the General Assembly of the United Nations which requested the Secretary-General to render the necessary assistance and to provide such services as may be required for the implemen-

tation of relevant parts of the Final Declaration,* the *Ad Hoc* Meeting has agreed that all information agreed to above should be provided in one of the authentic languages of the Convention and be sent to the United Nations Department for Disarmament Affairs and be promptly forwarded, in the form received, to all States Parties. Information should also be made available to the World Health Organization.

2. The *Ad Hoc* Meeting has agreed that the first exchange of information and data should take place as soon as possible and be sent to the United Nations Department for Disarmament Affairs not later than 15 October 1987. Thereafter information to be given on an annual basis should be provided not later than 15 April and should cover the previous calendar year.

3. The experts note that, should any question arise in relation to the objective of, or in the application of the provisions of, the Convention, including as regards the information and data which States Parties have undertaken to exchange, States Parties can make use of the provisions for consultation and co-operation under Article V of the Convention, using, *inter alia*, appropriate international procedures within the framework of the United Nations and in accordance with its Charter.

Attention was drawn to the possibility that, *inter alia*, the Secretary-General of the United Nations might be requested to investigate, with the assistance of qualified experts, following procedures available to him, information that may be brought to his attention concerning possible use of bacteriological (biological) or toxin weapons and that this possibility covers outbreaks of infectious diseases and similar occurrences caused by toxins, that seem to deviate from the normal pattern and that could be inter-

---

*In connection with the adoption of that resolution, the Secretariat of the United Nations issued a note (A/C.1/49) concerning the responsibilities entrusted to the secretary general under the resolution, stating that the secretary general considered that "he would be required to render technical services and assistance to States Parties to the Convention with a view to enabling them to implement relevant parts of the Final Declaration of the Review Conference, it being understood that such services and assistance would have no financial implications for the regular budget of the United Nations and that all related costs would be met by the States Parties to the Convention in accordance with the rules of procedure adopted by the Second Review Conference."

preted as resulting from the use of bacteriological (biological) or toxin weapons.

F. Additional Considerations

1. In addition to the modalities agreed to under items A–E the *Ad Hoc* Meeting considered, *inter alia*, proposals
   - that exchange of information should also cover research centres and laboratories which, in view of the type or scale of their activities involving highly pathogenic micro-organisms and/or toxins, could be considered relevant for the purpose of item A,
   - that exchange of information under item A should also cover research centres and laboratories which engage in field aerosol experiments with micro-organisms and toxins relevant to the Convention, or in research and development in the field of large scale bioprocessing specifically designed for highly pathogenic micro-organisms,
   - that exchange of information under item A could also occur on a voluntary basis with regard to research centres and laboratories engaged in research and development relevant to the Convention and related to the mechanism of transmission of micro-organisms and absorption and mode of action of toxins; toxicological assays; diagnostics and bio-sensors; and protective devices not elsewhere covered,
   - that experts also discuss including animal and plant diseases in the exchange of information,
   - that States Parties having national programmes for biological research should provide information on these programmes,
   - that States Parties should refrain from any discriminatory practices that may hamper the international peaceful co-operation in bioscience and in related basic and applied research, as well as international trade in related goods and equipment,
   - that exchange of data on outbreaks that seem to deviate from the normal pattern would be particularly important when the outbreak is associated with biological activities at a military facility.
   - that exchange of data on outbreaks that seem to deviate

from the normal pattern would be particularly important when the outbreak is associated with biological activities at any facility.

2. The *Ad Hoc* Meeting noted that with respect to items C and D it would be useful for States Parties to provide information on existing intergovernmental agreements that are relevant to the implementation of the commitments made in the Final Declaration.

3. Bearing in mind various proposals made, the *Ad Hoc* Meeting wishes to encourage States Parties to provide any additional information which they might consider useful to prevent or reduce the occurrence of ambiguities, doubts and suspicions and in order to improve international co-operation in the field of peaceful bacteriological (biological) activities.

4. Furthermore, the *Ad Hoc* Meeting is aware that the Third Review Conference shall consider, *inter alia*, the effectiveness of the co-operative measures agreed in the Final Declaration of the Second Review Conference and whether or not further actions are called for to create further co-operative measures in the context of Article V. In this regard States Parties may wish to take note of proposals presented during the *Ad Hoc* Meeting.

Appendix F:
Elements for a Verification Protocol

Article 1: Quantitative Constraints

Each state party undertakes not to research, develop, produce, otherwise acquire, stockpile, transfer, or retain any of the biological agents and toxins listed in the annex to this article for nonprohibited purposes in quantities larger than [x] grams.

Each state party undertakes to limit the capacity of equipment for production, harvesting, and long-term conservation of biological agents or toxins of every facility that is involved in protection and prophylaxis against possible hostile use of such agents or toxins, and handles one or more of the agents and toxins listed in the annex to this article, to a maximum of [to be defined].

Article 2: Transfer

Each state party undertakes not to transfer any of the biological agents and toxins listed in the annex to Article 1 of this protocol to a country that is not party to the convention.

Article 3: Declaration of Biological Agents and Toxins

Each state party will annually declare any research, development, production, acquisition, stockpiling, transfer, or retention of any of the biological agents and toxins listed in the annex to Article 1 of this protocol it plans in the coming calendar year.

Each state party will make an additional declaration if any change occurs in the plans declared in accordance with the first paragraph of this article.

The declarations on the basis of the first two paragraphs of this article will be made in accordance with the annex to this article. [In this annex the scope of the declarations and the procedural arrangements should be defined.]

Article 4: Declaration of Relevant Facilities

Each state party will, in accordance with the annex to this article, declare every facility within its jurisdiction or control that

1. has high containment facilities (as defined in the annex to this article), and/or
2. researches, develops, produces, or stockpiles any of the biological agents or toxins listed in the annex to this article, and/or
3. has production equipment with a combined capacity of x m^3 or more that is particularly suited for production of biological agents (to be defined in the annex to this article), and/or
4. has advanced equipment for harvesting biological agents (such as continuous-flow centrifuges and filtration techniques, to be defined in the annex to this article), and/or
5. has equipment for long-term storage of agents (such as freeze-drying equipment, to be defined in the annex to this article), and/or
6. has equipment for microencapsulation (capacity and details to be defined in the annex to this article), and/or
7. is involved in research and development for protection and prophylaxis against possible hostile use of biological agents or toxins.

Article 5: Routine Verification

Each facility declared under Article 4 of this protocol will be subject to routine international on-site verification in accordance with this article and its annex.

The purpose of routine on-site verification will be to verify the accuracy of the declarations made under Articles 3 and 4.

Each state party will every year nominate for inspection at least one and not more than [x] facilities declared under Article 4 of this protocol.

The [Inspectorate] will randomly select facilities for routine on-site inspection from the facilities nominated under this article.

Article 6: Challenge Inspections

Each state party has the right to request inspection of any location or facility under the jurisdiction or control of another state party, in order to clarify any matter which causes doubts about compliance with the Convention [to be modeled after the challenge inspection regime of the Chemical Weapons Convention].

Article 7: Inspection Procedures

All inspections according to this protocol will be conducted in accordance with the annex on the Protection of Confidential Information and the Protocol on Inspection Procedures. [Both could be modeled after the similar documents of the Chemical Weapons Convention.]

Article 8: Organization

The implementation of this protocol will be ensured by

* [the UN Department for Disarmament Affairs (might have to be reinforced for this purpose)] *or*
* [the Organization for the Prohibition of Biological Weapons (modeled after the Organization for the Prohibition of Chemical Weapons)] *or*
* [the Organization for the Prohibition of Chemical and Biological Weapons (this would require that the present Article 8 of the rolling text of the CWC be taken out of the draft convention and turned into the statute of an organization that would serve the purposes of both the BWC and the CWC)].

Annex to Article 1

1A. *List of Biological Agents*
   1. Anthrax
   2. Smallpox
   3. Tularemia
   4. –
1B. *List of Toxins*
   1. Saxitoxin
   2. Ricin
   3. Botulin toxin
   4. –
1C. *List of Organisms Capable of Producing Toxins on List 1B*
   1. –
   2. –
   3. –

Notes

The main sources for the history of the negotiations on the Biological Weapons Convention and on the ongoing negotiations on a Chemical Weapons Convention are the documents of the United Nations and of the Conference on Disarmament and its predecessors (see note 32, chap. 1). Most of these documents are available at the UN offices in New York and Geneva and at specialized libraries. The same is the case for the final documents of the review conferences. All official documents of the negotiations on a Chemical Weapons Convention in the Conference on Disarmament (documents CD/ . . . and verbatim records CD/PV . . .) and its Ad Hoc Committee on Chemical Weapons (documents CD/ CW/WP . . .) are regularly published by the Arms Control and Disarmament Division of the Canadian Department of External Affairs. The relevant UN documents have usually been published as documents of the General Assembly (documents A/ . . .) or the Security Council (documents S/ . . .). A factual overview of the discussions in the General Assembly and the Conference on Disarmament since 1976 is given in the United Nations Disarmament Yearbooks. The period before 1976 is covered by *The United Nations and Disarmament: 1945-1970* and *1970-1975*. The Netherlands Ministry of Foreign Affairs publishes yearly reports on the General Assembly of the United Nations *le (etc) Algemene Vergadering van de Verenigde Naties* and a (usually) biennial report on arms control negotiations *(Ontwapening, Veiligheid, Vrede* = Disarmament, Security, Peace). These books are written in Dutch, but they contain many documents in the original English version.

Many books on chemical weapons deal also with biological weapons, but the specialized literature on biological weapons and the efforts to ban them is rather small. Nicholas Sims has written the history of the First Review Conference (*The Diplomacy of Biological Disarmament: Vicissitudes of a Treaty in Force, 1975-1985* [London: Macmillan, 1988]) and many articles and brochures. The most up-to-date discussion of the yellow rain issue is probably the chapter "Yellow Rain in Southeast Asia: The Story Collapses" by Julian Robinson, Jeanne Guillemin, and Matthew Meselson in *Preventing a Biological Arms Race*, Susan Wright, ed. (Cambridge: MIT Press, 1990). A good overview can be found in "Sverdlovsk and Yellow Rain," by Elisa D. Harris in *International Security* 11, no. 4 (Spring 1987). A discussion of the agreed-upon confidence-building measures can be found in *Strengthening the Biological Weapons Convention by Confidence-Building Measures*, Erhard Geissler, ed., Stockholm International Peace Research Institute (SIPRI), Chemical and Biological Warfare Studies no. 10 (New York: Oxford University Press, 1989). SIPRI has also published several books that deal partly with biological weapons—e.g., the SIPRI yearbooks. *Preventing a Biological Arms Race* contains a lot of information and many thoughts and suggestions on the subject, as do the reports of the Federation of American Scientists: *Proposals for the Third Review Conference of the Biological Weapons Convention* and *Implementation of the Proposals for a Verification Protocol to the Biological Weapons Convention*. An indispensable source for facts is the *Arms Control Reporter*.

Introduction

1. Paragraph 17 of the report of July 1969. The official title of the report is *Chemical and Bacteriological (Biological) Weapons and the Effects of Their Possible Use* (documents A/7575 and S/9292).

Chapter 1

1. The use of poisons and poisoned bullets had been prohibited in the Hague conventions of 1899 and 1907. But not all major

powers were parties to these conventions, and during World War I the prohibition was severely undermined. The text of the new agreement, known as the Geneva Protocol of 1925, is added to this book as appendix A.

2. As of January 1, 1990, 125 countries were party to the Geneva Convention. About 50 of these countries have declared one or more reservations that are still valid. Ireland (1972), Australia (1986), New Zealand (1989), and the Czech and Slovak Federal Republic (1990) withdrew their reservations.

3. When ratifying the protocol in 1930 the Netherlands limited its reservation of the right of retaliation to the use of chemical weapons. When the United States ratified the protocol in 1975 it did likewise. All other parties that reserved the right of retaliation did so for both chemical and biological weapons. Countries that became party to the Biological Weapons Convention de facto lost their right to retaliate with biological weapons.

4. Some parties, such as the United States, have expressed their opinion that the Geneva Protocol does not cover tear gases and herbicides, but many others think differently.

5. As a result of the allegations of use of chemical weapons in Southeast Asia and Afghanistan and during the war between Iraq and Iran, the UN General Assembly requested the secretary general to devise procedures for effective investigation and to investigate any future reports (see section in this volume, "The Convention Threatened, 1980–1986," chap. 1).

6. On November 29, 1988, President François Mitterrand declared that the French biological weapons had been destroyed in 1972. See *Arms Control Reporter* 701.B.44. The Soviet Union has never officially acknowledged that it has at any time possessed a biological warfare capability, but neither has it denied it. It seems very probable that it had such capability before the entry into force of the convention. Germany started to prepare a biological warfare capability in 1942. Friedrich Hansen, "Zur Geschichte der deutschen biologischen Waffen," *1999: Zeitschrift für Sozialgeschichte des 20. und 21. Jahrhunderts*, no. 1 (1990).

7. See the speech of the British Under Secretary of State Michael Neubert on April 24, 1990, published in an information pack on Gruinard Island of the Chemical Defence Establishment, Porton Down.

8. Robert Harris and Jeremy Paxman, *A Higher Form of Killing* (St. Albans: Triad, 1983), p. xiii.

9. A comprehensive description of the Japanese biological warfare program is by Peter Williams and David Wallace, *Unit 731: Japan's Secret Biological Warfare in World War II* (New York: The Free Press, 1989).

10. See ibid., 73.

11. Ibid., 75.

12. Williams and Wallace (ibid.) base their story to a large extent on the reports of the trials in the Soviet Union of Japanese soldiers who had been involved in the Japanese biological warfare program. Although the tenor of the story is corroborated by other sources, it remains difficult to assess the reliability of the confessions reportedly made to the Soviet authorities by personnel involved in the Japanese program.

13. Ibid., 27.

14. Ibid., 26–29.

15. Ibid., 69.

16. Ibid., 91–93.

17. See Barton J. Bernstein, "Origins of the U.S. Biological Warfare Program," *Preventing a Biological Arms Race*, Susan Wright, ed. (Cambridge: MIT Press, 1990).

18. See figure 12.1 in Barton J. Bernstein, "The Birth of the U.S. Biological-Warfare Program," *Microorganisms: From Smallpox to Lyme Disease*, Thomas D. Brock, ed. (New York: W. H. Freeman and Company, 1990). The article was first published in *Scientific American*, June 1987.

19. Bernstein, "Origins of the U.S. Biological Warfare Program," 9.

20. Ibid., 14, 15.

21. Susan Wright, "Evolution of Biological Warfare Policy, 1945–1990," *Preventing a Biological Arms Race*, Susan Wright, ed. (Cambridge: MIT Press, 1990).

22. Ibid.

23. The five permanent members of the Security Council (China, France, the United Kingdom, the United States, and the Soviet Union) have the power of veto. But at that time the Republic of China (Taiwan) was still considered to represent China. The People's Republic of China was therefore not able to veto the action by the United Nations.

24. On December 23, 1952, for example, Radio Pjong Jang claimed that American airplanes had dropped thousands of infected spiders, bugs, and caterpillars above Chang Jonet and Ko-

song (according to Agence France Presse in Keesings Historisch Archief [Keesings Historical Archives], 10404).

25. According to Reuters, Dr. Brook Chisholm, director general of the World Health Organization, declared on April 3, 1952, that no evidence had been presented that bacteriological weapons had been used in Korea and that WHO did not have any indication that pointed to unusually large epidemics in North Korea or China (Keesings Historisch Archief, 9950).

26. The People's Republic of China was not yet a member, but the Soviet Union had ended its boycott of the Security Council.

27. UN Resolution 706, Art. 7. A remarkable aspect of the resolution was that the implementation of the organizational aspects of the investigation, such as transmitting the resolution to the governments concerned and reporting to the General Assembly, was not assigned to the secretary general, as is usual nowadays, but to the president of the General Assembly.

28. *The United Nations and Disarmament: 1945-1970* (New York: United Nations, 1970), 28.

29. It should be noted that until 1975 the United States was not party to the Geneva Protocol. When in 1975 the United States ratified the protocol, it made clear that, according to its interpretation, the scope of the protocol did not include tear gases and herbicides.

30. Following the example of UN publications, I have used the term "socialist countries" to designate the Soviet Union and its allies.

31. Statements of socialist countries at the UN General Assembly in 1967.

32. Document ENDC/231, August 6, 1968. Published in "Ontwapening, Veiligheid, Vrede 1966/68," Netherlands Ministry of Foreign Affairs, The Hague, 1969, p. 295. The Eighteen-Nation Disarmament Committee (ENDC) is the predecessor of the Conference on Disarmament (CD). The ENDC was instituted in 1961 as a replacement of the short-lived Ten-Nation Committee on Disarmament. The ENDC was composed of 5 (in practice 4, because France chose not to take part) Western and 5 Eastern European delegations (such as the Ten-Nation Committee on Disarmament) plus 8 neutral and nonaligned countries. The ENDC was in successive stages expanded to the current membership of 40 countries or 39 since the reunification of Germany (10 Western, 8 East-

ern [7 since reunification], 21 neutral and nonaligned, and China),
and it was renamed several times. In 1969 it became the Conference of the Committee on Disarmament (CCD), in 1978 the Committee on Disarmament (CD), and in 1984 the Conference on Disarmament (CD).

33. Paragraph 4 of the document.

34. Paragraph 7 of the document.

35. Paragraph 8 of the document. The United Kingdom did
not claim that verification of a ban on biological weapons would
be completely impossible. In that case it would have made little
sense to suggest that a body of experts would investigate allegations about noncompliance. It would seem that the United Kingdom meant to say that a system of routine verification that could
give complete certainty is impossible.

36. The statement was made in the ENDC on March 10,
1966, and was published in document ENDC/PV.247.

37. The Swedish delegate continued, saying: "If such a challenge, perhaps demanded by several parties, went unheeded – and
particularly if it went unheeded on several occasions – the case for
abrogating the treaty would seem to become particularly strong"
(ENDC/PV.247).

38. Paragraph 26 of the report of the ENDC of September 4,
1968, published as UN document A/7189.

39. Document A/7201/Add.1.

40. Resolution 2454 A (XXIII).

41. On July 1, 1969, the secretary general transmitted the
report to the General Assembly (A/7575), the Security Council (S/
9292), and the ENDC.

42. In the report the spread of DDT is used as an example of
how a toxic compound can eventually reach every place in the
world. This insecticide is found in many places in the world where
it has never been used, even in the tissue of penguins in Antarcti-
ca (para. 30 of the report).

43. Paragraph 375 of the report.

44. A revised version was submitted on August 26, 1969, as
document ENDC/255/Rev.1.

45. Article 3, paragraph 1.

46. Article 3, paragraph 2.

47. *Draft Convention on the Prohibition of the Development,
Production and Stockpiling of Chemical and Bacteriological (Bio-*

logical) Weapons and on the Destruction of Such Weapons. It was published as part of UN document A/7655.

48. In addition it covered only the weapons, not the agents, and did not cover equipment or other means to use biological agents.

49. After the ENDC was enlarged from 18 to 26 members in the summer of 1969, it was decided to change the name to the Conference of the Committee on Disarmament (CCD).

50. This declaration and the declaration of February 14, 1970, are reproduced in *Ontwapening, Veiligheid, Vrede, 1969/70* (Disarmament, Security, Peace), Netherlands Ministry of Foreign Affairs, 193 and 214. The text of National Security Memorandum 35 of November 25, 1969, was published as an appendix in *Preventing a Biological Arms Race*, Wright, ed.

51. On April 21, 1970, the United States submitted a working document to the CCD on toxins (CCD/286).

52. Document CCD/225/Rev.2 was introduced August 18, 1970.

53. The draft was published September 19, 1970, as part of A/8136.

54. Both were mentioned, for example, in a working document introduced by Yugoslavia in the CCD, August 6, 1970 (CCD/302).

55. Document CCD/300 of August 6, 1970, reproduced in *Ontwapening, 1969/70*, pp. 220–223.

56. Paragraph 5 of CCD/300.

57. The new proposal (CCD/325/Rev.1) was introduced March 30, 1971. It is reproduced in *Ontwapening, Veiligheid, Vrede 1971/73*, pp. 234–236.

58. According to the draft convention of the socialist countries, the Security Council could "undertake" (Art. 7, para. 2, CCD/325/Rev.1) investigations on the basis of complaints about noncompliance. Several states objected that the Security Council, being a political body, was not well suited for independent fact-finding. Such an investigation could be better conducted by an unbiased body, such as the secretary general of the United Nations or the World Health Organization. On the basis of the established facts, the Security Council could subsequently deliver a political judgment. The socialist countries were strongly opposed to such a procedure, which they considered an encroachment on

the privileges of the Security Council. The real reason probably was that it would deprive the Soviet Union of the power to veto the initiation of an unwelcome investigation.

59. Article 6, paragraph 2, of the convention.

60. Documents CCD/337 and CCD/338.

61. This final draft does not differ substantially from the final text of the convention added as an appendix to this book.

62. For a more complete and precise understanding of the Biological Weapons Convention, the reader is encouraged to consult the text of the convention that is added as appendix B.

63. According to Article 8, paragraph 2.

64. The People's Republic of China and France did originally not become party but eventually acceded. Several important countries in the Middle East are, however, still missing.

65. Verbatim records of the Conference of the Committee on Disarmament, CCD/PV.655.

66. Respectively on March 18, 1975 (CCD/PV.659), and June 24, 1975 (CCD/PV.666).

67. France decided not to participate in the negotiations because it objected to the bipolar setup of the Eighteen-Nation Disarmament Committee under the cochairmanship of the United States and the Soviet Union. The People's Republic of China had no seat in the ENDC because at that time Taiwan occupied the seat of China in the UN and other organizations such as the ENDC. France introduced a national law making it clear that France, although not a party, would comply with the norms of the convention.

68. For an extensive description and inside view of the course of this conference, the reader is referred to Nicholas A. Sims, *The Diplomacy of Biological Disarmament: Vicissitudes of a Treaty in Force, 1975–1985* (London: Macmillan, 1988).

69. The report was published as a document of the review conference, BWC/CONF.I/5.

70. The final declaration was recorded in the final document of the review conference, BWC/CONF.I/10. It is added as an appendix to this book.

71. The idea was inspired by the consultative committee provided for in the Environmental Modification Convention of 1977.

72. The numbering of the articles of the final declaration of a

review conference usually corresponds with the numbering of the articles of the treaty being reviewed. Both quotes are therefore from Article 5 of the final declaration.

73. Sims, *The Diplomacy of Biological Disarmament*, 136.

74. Information provided to the author.

75. See Matthew S. Meselson, "The Biological Weapons Convention and the Sverdlovsk Anthrax Outbreak of 1979," FAS Public Interest Report in *Journal of the Federation of American Scientists* 41, no. 7 (September 1988), and Elisa D. Harris, "Sverdlovsk and Yellow Rain: Two Cases of Soviet Noncompliance?" *International Security* 11, no. 4 (Spring 1987).

76. N. Bezrukov, anesthesiologist of Hospital No. 20 quoted in *Literaturnaya Gazeta*, no. 34. The article contains more alarming stories but no concrete evidence.

77. *Arms Control Reporter*, 701.B.38, 1988.

78. According to an article that was published in the *Uralsky Rabochy* daily in the spring of 1990, quoted in *Literaturnaya Gazeta*, no. 34.

79. Toxin weapons are also chemical weapons, but because they fall within the scope of the BWC, they are mentioned here specifically.

80. See, for example, T. D. Seeley, J. W. Nowicke, M. Meselson, J. Guillemin, and P. Akratanakul, "Yellow Rain," *Scientific American* 253, no. 3 (September 1985): 128–137; Harris, "Sverdlovsk and Yellow Rain," and J. J. Norman and J. G. Purdon, *Final Summary Report on the Investigation of "Yellow Rain" Samples from Southeast Asia* (Ottawa: Defence Research Establishment Ottawa report no. 912, February 1986).

81. The allegations were not limited to toxin agents but also included other types of chemical agents. Most attention, however, was given to the possible use of toxin agents. The question of whether other chemical agents have been used is in itself important but of less direct relevance for a discussion of compliance with the Biological Weapons Convention.

82. Vietnam, Cambodia, and Afghanistan became party in 1980, 1983, and 1986, respectively.

83. UN Resolution 35/144C was adopted on December 12, 1980, with 78 votes in favor, 17 against (including the socialist states), and 36 abstentions.

84. On December 9, 1981, by adoption of Resolution 36/96 C.

85. Vietnam had invaded Cambodia in 1978 and installed a pro-Vietnamese regime. The ousted Khmer Rouge then entered into a coalition with its non-Communist foes. This coalition under the leadership of Prince Norodom Sihanouk retained the seat of Cambodia in the United Nations, although it controlled only parts of the Cambodian countryside.

86. See paragraph 197 of the final report that was published as an annex to A/37/259.

87. See, for example, the report, commissioned by the Canadian Department of External Affairs by Dr. Bruno Schiefer, *Study of the Possible Use of Chemical Warfare Agents in Southeast Asia* (1982). The report could not confirm the reported attacks had taken place but noted that the reported events could not be explained on the basis of naturally occurring diseases. Most of the features described were consistent with trichothecene mycotoxosis, a disease that, according to Dr. Schiefer, did not naturally occur in Thailand and probably not in Laos or Cambodia either.

88. See Grant Evans, *The Yellow Rainmakers* (London: Verso Editions, 1983).

89. Julian Robinson, Jeanne Guillemin, and Matthew Meselson, "Yellow Rain in Southeast Asia: The Story Collapses," *Preventing a Biological Arms Race*, Wright, ed., 220–238.

90. Most of the alleged attacks in Laos in 1982 were reported to have taken place in the Phou Bia mountain area (see table 2 of the U.S. report published as a document of the First Committee of the 37th General Assembly of the United Nations, A/C.1/37/10). The author discussed the issue in April 1983 with a development worker that had been employed from 1979 to 1983 in a region of northern Laos (Nam Ngum) in the immediate Phou Bia vicinity. He had heard many stories about yellow rain, always from Hmong, never from lowland Laos. The usually secondhand stories ranged from airplanes that dropped canisters of powder from high altitudes to low-flying helicopters or biplanes that sprinkled white or yellow powders. Little was heard about casualties. Some chickens had fallen ill because of the yellow rain, and a fisherman who had used a canister of powder to kill fish had died himself after eating these fish. In a discussion with the author in August 1983, this report was confirmed by another development worker who had worked in the same area during the same time.

91. Resolution 37/98 D was adopted on December 13, 1982 by 86 against 19 votes and 33 abstentions.

92. The secretary general reported on his implementation of the resolution on October 2, 1984, in A/39/488.

93. Resolution 42/37 C of November 30, 1987.

94. The replies are contained in documents A/43/690 and Add.1; A/44/561 and Add.1, 2, and 3. The countries whose replies are contained in these documents are Australia, Austria, Belgium, Brazil, Brunei, Bulgaria, Canada, Central African Republic, Czechoslovakia, Denmark, Finland, France, Federal Republic of Germany, Iran, Iraq, Israel, Italy, Netherlands, New Zealand, Norway, Philippines, Spain, Sweden, Soviet Union, Tanzania, and the United States.

95. A/44/561.

96. The General Assembly adopted the resolution (Res. 37/98 C) on December 13, 1982, on the same date as it took note of the inconclusive report about the alleged use of chemical weapons in Southeast Asia and Afghanistan (Res. 37/98 E) and requested the secretary general to prepare for similar investigations in the future (Res. 37/98 D).

97. By note of July 17, 1983. The three depositary powers are the United Kingdom, the United States, and the Soviet Union.

98. Article 7 of the final declaration.

99. On April 24, 1984, in a note to the depositaries.

100. On July 30, 1984, in a note to the depositaries.

101. On December 12, 1984, the General Assembly adopted by consensus a resolution that noted that on the request of a majority of parties the Second Review Conference would take place in 1986.

102. The following is to a large extent based upon the personal experience of the author who took part both in the Second Review Conference and in the expert meeting in 1987.

103. BWC/CONF.II/4/ADD.2 of September 8, 1986, is reproduced in *Ontwapening, Veiligheid, Vrede 1985/86*, pp. 407–410; BWC/CONF.II/4/ADD.1 of August 29, 1986, and reproduced in *Ontwapening, Veiligheid, Vrede 1985/86*, pp. 411–419.

104. Agreement on confidence-building measures about containment facilities is hampered by the fact that no generally adopted definition of types of containment exists. The ad hoc meeting of experts based itself on the 1983 WHO *Laboratory*

Biosafety Manual. Usually four levels of containment are distinguished, designated as biosafety level 1 (BL1) or P1 (the lowest level: no special precautions) to BL4 or P4 (maximum containment). In practice, laboratory buildings are often provided with higher containment facilities than would officially be required according to WHO standards. See Geissler, ed., *Strengthening the Biological Weapons Convention*, 176–179, and paragraph 2 of the Soviet document.

105. The text of the final declaration of the review conference (that was published in the final document of the review conference, BWC/CONF.II/13) is included in this book as appendix D.

106. In Article 1 of the final declaration.

107. Article 2 speaks about "all agents, toxins, weapons, equipment and means of delivery specified in Article 1 of the Convention." For reasons of readability I will use the words "biological and toxin weapons."

108. Japan ratified the convention in June 1982.

109. Article 3, paragraph 1, of the final declaration.

110. In 1982 the Center for Disarmament was upgraded to UN Department for Disarmament Affairs.

111. Article 4, paragraph 3, of the final declaration.

112. Article 4, paragraph 4.

113. Article 5, paragraph 4, of the final declaration.

114. Article 5, paragraph 5.

115. In Article 5 of its final declaration.

116. The parallel between Article 5, paragraph 6, of the final declaration and Article 6 of the convention also extends to the undertaking of parties to cooperate with an investigation. In the last section of the sixth paragraph of Article 5 of its final declaration, the review conference considered that "States Parties shall co-operate with the consultative meeting . . . in clarifying ambiguous and unresolved matters, as well as co-operate in appropriate international procedures within the framework of the United Nations. . . . " This clause is vague and wordy but does seem to correspond to Article 6 of the convention in which parties undertake "to cooperate in carrying out any investigation which the Security Council may initiate."

117. Article 5, paragraph 6, section 2, of the final declaration.

118. Article 5, paragraph 7.

119. Article 10, paragraph 1, of the final declaration of the First Review Conference.

120. It is to be noted that this wording only prohibits non-proliferation measures to be "used to impose restrictions" on transfer for peaceful purposes. It does not prohibit measures that unintentionally have such effects.

121. It also should be noted that the words have been taken from the first paragraph of Article 10 and, as has been pointed out above, do not explicitly deal with the exchange of biological agents and toxins and do not mention processing and production of these agents.

122. The undertaking of parties under Article 10 of the convention to contribute to such cooperation is similar to the undertaking under Article 9 to continue negotiations in good faith on a chemical weapons ban. Both undertakings are part of the convention and are legally binding upon all parties, but their actual implementation falls outside the scope of the convention and the review conferences. It is therefore remarkable that the Second Review Conference went into so much detail about peaceful cooperation. It is difficult to imagine that the review conference could have gone into the same level of detail in its recommendations for the negotiations on a chemical weapons ban, without running into political trouble.

123. This somewhat curious wording (Art. 12, para. 1, of the final declaration) might give the impression that if by 1991 no majority of parties would have asked for a review conference, no such conference would take place. In the autumn of 1990 the General Assembly of the United Nations decided to hold the conference from September 9 to 30, 1991.

124. The official name of the meeting was Ad Hoc Meeting of Scientific and Technical Experts from States Parties to the Convention on the Prohibition of the Development, Production, and Stockpiling of Bacteriological (Biological) and Toxin Weapons and on Their Destruction.

125. Australia, Canada, the Federal Republic of Germany, the Netherlands, Sweden, the United Kingdom, and the United States were the seven parties that presented data. The presentation of these data also could be considered as response to Article 5, paragraph 9, of the final declaration of the review conference in which parties, pending the results of the ad hoc meeting of scien-

tific and technical experts, were urged to report the data agreed upon to the UN Department for Disarmament Affairs.

126. The English original of the report was published April 21, 1987, BWC/CONF.II/EX/2.

127. Part F, paragraph 3, of the modalities for the exchange of information, BWC/CONF.II/EX/2, chapter 2.

128. An example of the latter is the Department of Microbiology of the Medical Biological Laboratory TNO in the Netherlands. This laboratory is partly financed by the Netherlands Ministry of Defense and is, among other things, involved in study of prophylaxis and protection against microbial aerosols. As the department does not have any containment units, it did not have to be reported. It should be noted, however, that the department is collocated with a laboratory with P3 containment facilities. This laboratory is not involved in protection or prophylaxis and therefore also does not have to be declared. In the view of the Netherlands government, however, declaration of all defense-funded biological laboratories and of all P3 laboratories, certainly when they are collocated with defense-related laboratories, would be useful as a confidence-building measure. Both laboratories were therefore reported as a confidence-building measure.

129. See part B, paragraph 1, of the modalities.

130. This background information should be given to the UN Department for Disarmament Affairs (see note to para. 2). Organisms that can cause disease are classified in four risk groups.

131. Part E, paragraph 3, of the modalities.

132. Part C, paragraph 1, of the modalities.

133. Part C, paragraph 2, of the modalities.

134. Part C, paragraph 3, of the modalities.

135. Part B, paragraph 5, of the modalities.

136. Part B, paragraph 4, of the modalities.

137. First section of the third paragraph of part E of the agreed-upon modalities.

138. Footnote to paragraph 1 of part E of the modalities. The secretary general's view is found in A/C.1/41/9.

139. All written proposals are included in an attachment to the report of the meeting.

140. *Jane's Defense Weekly*, January 14, 1989, quoted in the *Arms Control Reporter*, 701.B.47.

141. Statement of Thomas J. Welch, deputy assistant to the

secretary of defense, in a hearing on biological warfare testing on May 3, 1988, before the Subcommittee on Arms Control, International Security and Science of the Committee on Foreign Affairs, the Subcommittee on Energy and Environment of the Committee on Interior and Insular Affairs, and the Subcommittee on Military Installations and Facilities of the Committee on Armed Services, 34.

142. *The Observer*, March 27, 1988.

143. Reuters from Washington on January 18, 1989, reporting on ABC News of January 17 and 18.

144. Five hundred milligrams of T-2 toxin and 100 milligrams of HT-2 toxin. See the *Arms Control Reporter*, 701.B.49.

145. Senator John McCain in the U.S. Senate on January 25, 1989, quoted by David Ottaway in *Washington Post*, January 26 and 29, 1989. See the *Arms Control Reporter*, 701.B.49.

146. According to intelligence reports disclosed on September 28, 1990, by Les Aspin, chairman of the House Armed Services Committee (*International Herald Tribune*, September 28–29, 1990).

147. According to the Tunisian newspaper *Al Sabah* as quoted by Reuters in the *International Herald Tribune*, November 6, 1990.

148. Reuters from Washington, D.C., January 18, 1989, quoted by ABC News on the same day.

149. Reuters from Nicosia, October 19, 1988.

150. Reuters from Washington, D.C., January 18, 1989.

151. *New York Times*, August 13, 1989, quoted in *Arms Control Reporter*, 701.B.51.

152. The Australian group is an informal group of industrialized countries under Australian chairmanship. It was started in 1984 in reaction to the use of chemical weapons in the Iran-Iraq War, to coordinate national measures to prevent proliferation of chemical and biological weapons.

153. According to U.S. officials quoted in the *New York Times* article, the United States had urged the Netherlands to block the sale. In fact the United States was not involved in the information exchange between Canada and the Netherlands and was informed by the Netherlands government after the Netherlands had decided that such cultures should not be exported to Iran. The author was personally involved in the handling of these matters. Because of the sensitive character of the events, the

description is mainly based on what has surfaced in the press. Some relevant details have, however, been added.

154. According to some specialists in the field, mycotoxins might be used for development of an agent against AIDS (oral remarks to the author).

155. Rijksinstituut voor Volksgezondheid en Milieuhygiene or RIVM (Institute for Public Health and Environmental Protection).

156. The affair became public at the beginning of 1990. "Bedrijf leverde Iran apparaat voor bio-wapens" (Company supplied Iran equipment for biological weapons), *NRC Handelsblad*, January 31, 1990, p. 3.

157. Bringing the item under formal export controls might have helped in future cases, but as laws do not apply retrospectively, it would have been difficult to stop the order (which had been already partly paid for) in this way.

Chapter 2

1. The facts and opinions described in this chapter are based on the discussions the author had between 1986 and 1990 with scientists and other people involved in biotechnology.

2. Toxin weapons are possibly more promising in this respect than microbial and viral agents, as some of these weapons might combine the advantages of chemical weapons (no danger of contagion through infection) and biological weapons (possibility of prophylaxis of one's own troops).

3. To be effective, a biological agent should remain active until it reaches its intended victims. After that it should become inactive as soon as possible as opposed to the case of Gruinard Island. On this island near the British coast, the United Kingdom experimented with anthrax. Parts of the island remained contaminated for about 45 years after the experiments.

4. Geissler, ed., *Strengthening the Biological Weapons Convention*, 18.

5. DNA recombination could possibly be used to accelerate the expression of a toxic property of an agent or to inhibit an organism from producing spores. See J. Jelsma, "Betekenis van ontwikkelingen in de civiele biotechnologie voor militair gebruik" ("Significance of developments in civil biotechnology for military use"), *Transaktie* 1989/2, pp. 164–177.

6. The difference between these judgments might be partly

explained by the point the authors try to make. Whereas Geissler seems driven by the fear that the risks involved in the development of biotechnology will be underestimated, Pugwash seems primarily preoccupied by the possibility that some nations might get interested in acquiring a biological (retaliatory) capability. The quotation is from *Pugwash Newsletter*, October 1989, p. 81.

7. See *Arms Control Reporter*, 701.B.48. In a few cases, individuals have threatened to use biological warfare agents.

8. As biological agents do exist and reproduce themselves, development of biological warfare agents differs from development of new chemical warfare agents.

9. A chemical agent also has to be conserved, of course, but the problems involved are of a different order.

10. The main reason for the lack of civil applications is the high toxicity of the agents. If they are nevertheless used, it is often to treat otherwise incurable diseases, such as cancer and AIDS. Mustard gas, for example, is sometimes used against certain skin diseases.

11. The criterion is whether an agent is used against animals or plants to harm the animal or plant or to harm the person who uses the animal or plant. Use of a biological agent to harm a pathogenic organism could be considered a kind of biological warfare, but it is not covered by the Biological Weapons Convention.

12. The Biological Weapons Convention does not prohibit development, production, and stockpiling of biological agents for prophylactic and protective purposes.

13. In other fields the scale of research can sometimes be very large. A good example from high-energy physics is the 27-kilometer-long tunnel made for the European Center for Nuclear Research (CERN) near Geneva.

14. *Soviet Military Power 1984*, p. 73.

15. In the rolling text (the draft convention that is periodically revised) of February 1, 1990 (CD/961, p. 10), two alternative texts for a provision in Article 1 are within brackets (which means that no provisional agreement has been reached on inclusion in the convention).

16. Article 1, paragraph 5, of the final declaration.

17. Hostile use of herbicides is forbidden, however, by the Environmental Modification Convention of 1977 if its effects are widespread, severe, or long-lasting.

18. The phrase "peaceful purposes" is a notorious example of an expression that gradually has lost most of its original mean-

ing. Article 88 of the Law of the Sea, for example, stipulates: "The high seas shall be reserved for peaceful purposes." On the face of it, it would seem that warships would no longer be allowed on the high seas, but that is not the case. In this article, the term "peaceful" means no more than "not for aggressive purposes."

19. The rolling text of the Chemical Weapons Convention of August 1983 still speaks about "medical, law enforcement, or other peaceful purposes" (CD/416, Annex 1, p. 3, August 22, 1983). In August 1984 this clause was set within brackets and an alternative text (also within brackets) was given, in which the sequence of the words is changed slightly, but significantly: "medical or other peaceful purposes, law enforcement" (CD/539, Annex 1, p. 6, of August 28, 1984). In 1985 the only text remaining was "medical or other peaceful purposes, domestic law enforcement purposes" (CD/636, appendix 1, 7, August 23, 1985).

20. Article 2, paragraph 5, of the rolling text. See CD/1033, p. 26.

21. Last section of Article 2, paragraph 1 (CD/1033, p. 23).

22. Geissler, ed., *Strengthening the Biological Weapons Convention.*

23. Article 5, paragraph 9, of the final declaration.

24. Article 5, paragraph 7, first part of the final declaration of the Second Review Conference.

25. This definition is given in Geissler, ed., *Strengthening the Biological Weapons Convention*, 150.

26. Later editions of the rolling text of the draft Chemical Weapons Convention avoid the words "permitted purposes" and use "purposes not prohibited under the convention" instead. CD/416, Annex 1, p. 3.

27. TASS in FBIS-SU, March 2, 1989, quoted in the *Arms Control Reporter*, 701.B.50.

28. Chinese, English, French, Russian, and Spanish.

29. Report of Associated Press in the *New York Times*, December 3, 1989.

30. D'Vera Cohn in the *Washington Post*, March 22, 1990, p. A15.

31. Carol N. Levitt in the *Washington Post*, December 13, 1989.

32. This explanation was given to the author by a member of the Soviet delegation to the Conference on Disarmament. In April 1990, however, the United Kingdom in its annual declaration in-

formed other parties that an outbreak of Q-fever in and around east Birmingham, mainly among males of working age, might fall under the reporting guidelines.

Chapter 3

1. "Capability" is a confusing term because it is used with different meanings. What it means here is not that a chemical plant would be ready to start producing chemical warfare agents but that a plant could be used for that purpose after minor or major, but usually time-consuming and costly, alterations.

2. Binary nerve agents contain two components that, when mixed, react and form a chemical warfare agent. Until the moment of delivery, the two relatively nontoxic components are kept separate, which facilitates transport, storage, and handling.

3. During a production process, 1 to 10 percent of a chemical compound might be "lost" for a number of reasons such as different calibrations of measuring instruments, residues in pipes, and so on. Consequently it is very difficult to verify by means of some sort of material accounting system whether 1 percent of the total production is embezzled for chemical weapons purposes. This means that, if we assume that 100 agent tons is a militarily relevant quantity, verification of nonproduction of chemical warfare agents through material accountancy is not practical if the quantity produced is 10,000 tons or more.

4. Paul Fildes, in UK Public Record Offices file DEFE 1/1251 and DEFE 2/1252, quoted by J. P. Perry Robinson in table 3 accompanying his unpublished speaking notes for the Noordwijk biological weapons seminar, February 6–8, 1991.

5. G. A. Deshazer, *BW Potential for the Snark Missile*, U.S. Army Chemical Corps Research & Development Command Biological Warfare Laboratories Technical Study 20, Fort Detrick, January 1960 (AD 322516), quoted by J. P. Perry Robinson in unpublished notes.

6. For a comparison between verification of nonproduction of nuclear weapons and verification of nonproduction of chemical weapons, see Barend ter Haar and Piet de Klerk, "Verification of Non-Production: Chemical and Nuclear Weapons Compared," *Arms Control*, December 1987.

7. As in the case of the treaty for the Prohibition of Nuclear Weapons in Latin America, Article 16.

8. The full title is *Document of the Stockholm Conference on Confidence- and Security-Building Measures and Disarmament in Europe Convened in Accordance with the Relevant Provisions of the Concluding Document of the Madrid Meeting of the Conference on Security and Co-operation in Europe.* The relevant paragraphs are 63 through 96.

9. Article 74 of the document.

10. In case of amphibious landing or a parachute assault; otherwise at least 13,000 troops should be involved (Art. 31).

11. Bush introduced the concept of challenge inspections that can never be refused in his speech to the Conference on Disarmament in Geneva in 1984, when he introduced the U.S. draft Chemical Weapons Convention.

12. Verification might become very complicated if the party would decide not to destroy its biological and toxin weapons, but to convert them to peaceful purposes (although it is very hard to think of a peaceful purpose to which they could be converted). Precisely because of the difficulty of verifying such conversion, the CWC will not allow conversion of chemical weapons to peaceful purposes. The BWC, however, was not designed with a view to verification; we will note this again and again when we analyze the requirements for effective verification. Yet it seems very unlikely that a country would accede to the convention before destroying its stocks of biological weapons.

13. The reason for this apparent omission was probably that the equipment used for the production (or, rather, reproduction) of biological weapons was of a general, multipurpose character. When destroyed it could have been relatively easily replaced by equipment used to produce biological agents of toxins for nonprohibited purposes. An obligation to destroy the production equipment would therefore not have contributed much to confidence in compliance.

14. The annex on chemicals forms part of the rolling text of the Chemical Weapons Convention. See pp. 58–76 of CD/1033.

15. Annex 1 to Article 6, "General Provisions," paragraph 1 (CD/1033, p. 122).

16. In a footnote to the rolling text, a view was expressed "that ultratoxic substances (to be determined) shall not be allowed to be produced in excess of 10 g per year" (CD/1033, p. 123).

17. For the projected verification regime for single small-scale facilities, see Annex 1 to Article 6 of the rolling text, chapter on single small-scale facilities (CD/1033, pp. 125, 126). For the projected verification regime for the facilities mentioned under *b* and *c*, see the same annex, section on facilities covered by paragraph 2 of the section on production above (CD/1033, pp. 128, 129).

18. It would, for example, be possible to decide that certain activities would have to be declared and inspected, without regard to whether the official purpose was called research or development.

19. CD/1033, pp. 77–82.

20. For details see the rolling text of the draft convention article 13 amendments and the annex on chemicals, part 4, "Modalities for Revision of Schedules and Guidelines" (CD/1033, pp. 49–51, 69–71).

Chapter 4

1. At the time of this writing, the Federation of American Scientists (FAS) working group had not finalized these reports. The final versions of *Proposals for the Third Review Conference of the Biological Weapons Convention* and *Implementation of the Proposals for a Verification Protocol to the Biological Weapons Convention* were published in October 1990 and February 1991 respectively. Copies of these reports can be obtained from the Federation of American Scientists, Washington, D.C.

2. Under this article parties undertook "to facilitate . . . the fullest possible exchange of equipment, materials and scientific and technological information" for the use of biological agents and toxins for peaceful purposes. The Second Review Conference urged parties to take specific measures to this end "through their active intervention" and listed a number of possible measures (Art. 10 of the final declaration).

3. The author, for example, who was until 1989 responsible for the data provided by the Netherlands, once received handwritten information on one of the institutes of the Netherlands. To expedite delivery of the data, he faxed the information in the form received to the Netherlands permanent representation to the UN in New York with the request to forward the data to the UN

Department of Disarmament Affairs. The fax was handed over to a UN official, photocopied, and in the photocopied handwriting, distributed to all parties. This was a minor thing, but it probably did not stimulate reading.

4. See the note (A/C.1/41/9) issued by the UN secretariat in connection with the adoption of resolution 41/58 A, which requested the secretary general to provide services required to implement the final declaration.

5. The list is based on discussions with experts in the fields of toxicology, microbiology, and biotechnology. The list does not have any pretention of being complete but is offered as a basis for discussion.

6. FAS, *Proposals for the Third Review Conference*, "Long-Term Proposal," C.3.

7. Up until 1989 about 120 facilities were declared. Only about half of them did, strictly speaking, have to be declared.

8. See paragraph [11.3.2].

9. FAS, *Proposals for the Third Review Conference*, "Short-Term Proposal," Article 1, proposal A.

Index

Afghanistan: chemical weapons in, 22, 23–24, 161n.5; party to Biological Weapons Convention, 167n.82

AIDS, 29, 173–74n.154

animal diseases, 3, 68–69, 175n.11; information exchange and, 153; Japanese research and, 4

anthrax, 158; Iraq and, 49; Japan and, 4, 5; militarily relevant quantity, 82; Sverdlovsk epidemic, 20–22; U.K. and, 4, 174n.3; U.S. research during World War II and, 6

Antonov, Nikolai, 22

applied research, 43, 64–65, 150

Arafat, Yasir, 49

arms control, costs of, 102

assistance, to party exposed to danger, 119

Australian group, 52–53, 173n.152

bacteriological weapons, 3, 10, 11, 15–16

basic research, unclassified, 43, 150

binary nerve agents, 78, 177n.2

biological arms control, history of, 1–53

biological chemicals, 28

biological warfare: controllable, 55; increased risk of, 112

biological weapons: acquiring versus using, 59–62; conservation of, 60; defined, xxi; effectiveness of, 60; growing threat of, 54–58; law enforcement and, 69; literature on, 160n.; militarily relevant quantity, 60, 81, 82, 89, 92, 93; military training and, 66–67; new and improved agents, 55–56; new production technologies, 56–57; preparation for use, 66–67; production requirements, 51; production steps, 59; reproducing in victim, 60; route from possession to use, 61; slow effects of, 1; tactical utility of, xvii, 60–61; verifying destruction of, 86; as weapons of terror, 57, 100

Biological Weapons Convention (Convention on the Prohibition of the Development, Production,

rations of, 90–91; dual-purpose,
80–81; exchange of, 36; hazardous materials handling and, 51;
most risky, 90–91; multipurpose,
178n.13; production requirements, 51; reasons for concern
about, 104–5
experts, ad hoc meeting of (1987),
38–48, 70, 136, 143–54
export controls, 51, 52, 53, 100

facilities, declaration of, 156. *See
also* laboratories
fact-finding, 18–19
Federation of American Scientists,
99, 105, 179n.1
fermenters, 51, 53, 60, 104
field aerosol experiments, 153
filtration techniques, 104
France: biological warfare capability, 4; biological weapons destroyed, 161n.6; Eighteen-Nation Disarmament Committee
and, 166n.67; information exchange and, 71; unwilling to be
party to Convention, 17
freeze-drying equipment, 105
fungal cultures, 52–53

Geissler, Erhard, 56
genetic engineering, 17, 18, 28,
132
Geneva Protocol (1925), xvii, 100,
114–15, 119, 127, 137; Biological
Weapons Convention versus, 58;
chemical weapons and, 2; confidence building and verification
and, 3; herbicides and, 161n.4,
163n.29; scope of, 2–3; shortcomings of, 2–3, 15; talks about
amendments to, 9; tear gases
and, 161n.4, 163n.29; U.S. and,
12, 163n.29; worldwide application, 3

Germany, biological warfare capability, 4, 161n.6
glanders, Japan and, 4
Gruinard Island, 4, 174n.3

Hague conventions (1899, 1907),
160–61n.1
Haig, Alexander, 24
Halabja, bombing of, 57
harvesters, 51, 52, 104
Hashemi-Rafsanjani, Ali Akbar, 50
hazardous materials, equipment
for handling, 51
herbicides, 161n.4, 163n.29,
175n.17
Hmong, yellow rain and, 23, 24,
168n.90
hydrogen cyanide, 79

immunization: against biological
weapons, 61; research and, 12–13
implementation, national measures for, 32–33
imports, 61, 62. *See also* export
controls
infectious disease research, 71
information exchange, xviii, 119–
20, 128, 133, 136; active promotion of contacts and, 44–45; ad
hoc meeting of experts and, 38–
45, 143–54; confidentiality and,
96–97, 111; costs and, 47; disease outbreaks and, 34–35, 38,
40–42, 45, 146–48, 152; encouragement to publish and, 42–44;
feedback on, 103; improving,
102, 179–80n.3; laboratories and,
34, 38, 39–40, 143–45; need for
increased, 107–8; participation
in, 48, 70, 101; peaceful purposes
and, 36; private institutes and
companies and, 105; procedures
for, 45; research and, 35, 39–40,
143–45; Sverdlovsk and, 22; UN